CW00340274

WHAT PEOPLE ARE SAYIN

A shot of adrenaline with words, designed to trigger an awakening to your own superpowers and Divinity.

Dr. Joe Vitale, author, "Zero Limits," "The Miracle;"
star in the hit movie "The Secret"

If you are feeling stuck, frustrated, unhappy or simply anxious about life in general and you don't know why, then you have found your way to the perfect solution. UNSTUCK is a practical and heartfelt guide that not only explains why you're feeling stuck, it also gives you the blueprint on how to thrive regardless of your situation or the world around you.

Natalie Ledwell, Best Selling Author,
Co-Founder Mind Movies

UNSTUCK provides guidance in a world where old paradigms aren't working anymore. This work works! I love the blend of practical advice and deep spiritual wisdom.

Christine Hassler, Expectation Hangover

UNSTUCK *is a practical guide from an elevated perspective that will awaken and shift you from barely surviving in this rapidly changing world to the blissful freedom of thriving. Run, don't walk to get your copy NOW! Bravo, Jennifer!"*

Lisa Winston, #1 Bestselling Author of
Your Turning Point

UNSTUCK *provides the missing piece in a world where the old paradigms just aren't working anymore. The brilliant Jennifer Hough is the ideal person to guide us all to a new level of empowerment and a better, truer way to live.*

Debra Poneman
Bestselling author and founder, Yes to Success, Inc.

UNSTUCK *provides the missing piece in a world where old paradigms aren't working anymore. This works. So good!*

Tracey Samlow Star

Wow! I am so energized and activated after reading **UN**STUCK *by Jennifer Hough. The chapter about becoming a master at receiving, along with the one about expanding my financial success, helped reconnect me to my natural state of being—open to both request and receive what makes me happy and moves me forward—in several areas of my life. I love the well-written discussions, stories, and explanations followed by clear steps to help me practice staying aligned with flow. If you are ready to claim your next level of possibilities with ease, whether you have been feeling stuck or not, this book can help you get there.*

Wini Curley, PhD

I absolutely LOVED reading it!!

"Our body loves us so much it will never lie. It is our greatest guide. When we get symptoms of dis-ease, it's like being told the painful truth by our most faithful friend. It might be painful to hear such a truth coming from such a trusted companion, but in hearing it, we can more deeply appreciate the friend as well as take enthusiastic action to deal with the problem." (Excerpt from *UNSTUCK*)

Like wow!!! I cannot wait to read the rest of the book when it comes out!! "

Dr. Marie-Andree Nowlan, ND,
Naturopathic Doctor

UNSTUCK

THE PHYSICS OF GETTING OUT OF YOUR OWN WAY

JENNIFER HOUGH

UNSTUCK
The Physics of Getting Out of Your Own Way
Jennifer Hough

Published by I Fly Publishing, Asheville, NC

Project Management and Book Design: DavisCreativePublishingPartners.com

Cover: Kelly Pasholk, yourbookdesigned.com

Cover art: by Daniel B. Holeman, AwakenVisions.com

Editors: Susan Crossman, CrossmanCommunications.com, Julia Petrisor, Wini Curley, PhD, with special contributions by Lois Lenarduzzi

Library of Congress Cataloging-in-Publication Data

Library of Congress Control Number: 2021925099

Jennifer Hough

UNSTUCK: The Physics of Getting Out of Your Own Way

ISBN: 979-8-9854505-0-7 (paperback)
979-8-9854505-1-4 (ebook)

BISAC Subject headings:

1. OCC012000   Body, mind and spirit/mysticism
2. FAM013000   Family and relationship/conflict resolution
3. PSY045000   Psychology/movements/general

2022

Dedicated to my dear friend Judith Onley,
who decided that her powers are best used from
a place where her spirit is not limited by a body.

You are missed, and yet I feel you here
in every word, Angel.

DISCLAIMER

The information provided by Jennifer Hough ("we," "us" or "our") is for general informational purposes only. All information in the book is provided in good faith, however we make no representation or warranty of any kind, express or implied, regarding the accuracy, adequacy, validity, reliability, availability or completeness of any information I'm the book. UNDER NO CIRCUMSTANCE SHALL WE HAVE ANY LIABILITY TO YOU FOR ANY LOSS OR DAMAGE OF ANY KIND INCURRED AS A RESULT OF THE USE OF THE SITE OR RELIANCE ON ANY INFORMATION PROVIDED ON THE SITE. YOUR USE OF AND YOUR RELIANCE ON ANY INFORMATION IN THE BOOK IS SOLELY AT YOUR OWN RISK.

EXTERNAL LINKS DISCLAIMER

The book contains (or you may be sent through the book) links to other websites or content belonging to or originating from third parties or links to websites and features in banners or other advertising. Such external links are not investigated, monitored, or checked for accuracy, adequacy, validity, reliability, availability or completeness by us. WE DO NOT WARRANT, ENDORSE, GUARANTEE, OR ASSUME RESPONSIBILITY FOR THE ACCURACY OR RELIABILITY OF ANY INFORMATION OFFERED BY THIRD-PARTY WEBSITES LINKED THROUGH THE BOOK OR ANY WEBSITE OR FEATURE. WE WILL NOT BE A PARTY TO OR IN ANY WAY BE RESPONSIBLE FOR MONITORING ANY TRANSACTION BETWEEN YOU AND THIRD-PARTY PROVIDERS OF PRODUCTS OR SERVICES.

PROFESSIONAL DISCLAIMER

The book cannot and does not contain medical/health advice. The medical/health information is provided for general informational and educational purposes only and is not a substitute for professional advice. Accordingly, before taking any actions based upon such information, we encourage you to consult with the appropriate professionals. We do not provide any kind of medical/health advice. THE USE OR RELIANCE OF ANY INFORMATION CONTAINED ON THIS BOOK IS SOLELY AT YOUR OWN RISK.

TABLE OF CONTENTS

ACKNOWLEDGMENTS

It takes a village to create a book that encapsulates so much in so few pages. It takes special people to come and play in such an energized, creative, and ever-changing vortex. The tenacity and heart of everyone involved in this project are deeply appreciated.

My heart is full as I acknowledge the people who were absolute champions for me getting this book done with integrity while ensuring that my heart was consistently in the right place.

Adam Lamb, my sweet hubby, methodically took my spoken words and grounded them with love and commitment into writing. Your creative ability and profound writing skills inspired me in a way I cannot describe. That you would do such a great job with the bones of this book when all it did was overwhelm me is a true gift. It wouldn't have happened without you. Thank you.

Jeannie Selda, who has been beside me from the beginning of The Wide Awakening, for encouraging me, seeing me, loving me back into getting this done. No words…just gratitude forever for your friendship and neutrality.

Susan Crossman, of Crossman Communications, sat with me while I wrote and structured the first pass to create this book. She then took time at the last minute to make sure this baby would be birthed well. Susan is an influential author in her own right and an editor of epic proportions. I am so blessed to have you at my side, encouraging me with such heart. Thank you.

Deep appreciation to Jennifer Conaway, who cracked a feather whip and stayed committed to completing this project in an inspiring way. She believed in this from the get-go and refused to accept any excuses while encouraging the team and me the whole time. Thank you, JC; now I know your superpowers even better!

Julia Petrisor, an excellent editor who stepped in at the last minute to get this book complete and out the door. Your playful spirit, easygoing nature, willingness to say yes, and skills are forever appreciated.

Kay Ross, who is my new detail queen, deserves many thanks. I don't know what you put in your tea over there on the other side of the world, but my gosh, you have to send me some. I want that kind of energy, clarity, and attention to detail too! This is yet another one of the dozens of thank-yous I have already expressed, and I mean every one of them.

Elizabeth Doty, who has been on our team for years, is a technical editor and also edits our emails. Her contribution to all things written for The Wide Awakening is in my heart. She picked up the details I left off for the first four chapters. It wouldn't have happened without you.

Susannah Hansen made sure the house was in order and read some chapters to ensure I was on the right track, while the rest of the team members were relentless champions for all the details happening in the company while I wrote. Don't know where this book would be without you. Oops, yes, I do. It wouldn't have gotten done! Thank you.

Nadine, thank you for keeping me on track and ensuring my world was in order while I immersed myself in the book writing process. So blessed.

The team at Davis Creative just rocks. Again, so blessed by your patience and flexibility. Deep appreciation to you.

On the editing front, I am so grateful to Denise Conte, Wini Curley, and Lois Lenarduzzi for stepping in and stepping up to help me when I had no idea how this was going to get done on time. Honestly, again, no idea what I would do without you all. Thank you for being so detailed in areas that I am not.

To my current clients, I adore you. Your courage inspires me to keep going every day. Your stories are the reason for this book. Thank you for giving me such a blessed and meaningful life. Keep thriving and being an example of what is possible. Everything is changing. Thank you.

To my adorable parents, who will get the first copies of this book. You gave me a powerful foundation of values and taught me to care about others, to be a leader, and to create a body of work based on the life that started with you. You both do so much for your community and always have. This is my attempt to follow in those footsteps. I love you.

To the Evolutionary Business Council, Teresa de Grosbois and Pam Bayne, for all you've done to support, cheerlead, and continue to expand what is possible for leaders and their ability to make a difference in the world. My life would have been very different without you.

To every teacher, healer, scientist, doctor, shaman, and the like that ever touched my life, you are all here somehow. Your wisdom and processes gave me the ability to hear beyond words. Thank you.

And finally, to my guides, including dear, dear William Linville and his wife, Mary. What do I even say? My life is blissfully unfolding in directions I never knew it would take, in great part because of you. You have made my life more delicious than I alone could have imagined.

FOREWORD

By Susan Crossman

Standing at the front of the community hall and hearing the words of blessing the senior elders of New Zealand's Waitaha Nation sing over me, I feel swept into the sequence of miracles that brought me to this profound moment.

The Waitaha—the People of Peace—are inviting me to keep a sacred appointment that was to change the entire trajectory of my life. They are entrusting me with their Truth. Not too many years earlier, I had been overwhelmed by the responsibility that I felt came with being the self-employed widowed mother of three gleeful children who took the concept of "coloring outside the lines" to frightening new heights. I also had a disabled elderly mother to care for. I had been beset by my past and worried about my future. I was firmly rooted in urban Canada. So, how had I ended up *here,* on tribal lands *in New Zealand of all places*?!

The wisdom of Jennifer Hough is how.

Scant years after my husband passed away, I found myself struggling to make sense of a life that had been full of trauma and woe. I synchronistically found myself in Jennifer's Get Out of Your Own Way™ program one day but, to be honest, didn't think I was *in* my own way at the time. Life had dealt me nuclear lemons. I was dealing with the lemons the best way I could. And in my independent-outthink-disaster-kind-of-way, although I was miserably unhappy, I figured I was doing pretty well. Until one of my girlfriends dragged me along to Get Out of Your Own Way™. Intrigued, the insights and peace that came through that program inspired me to take another one of Jennifer's programs.

It felt good to be waking up.

I took The Wide Awakening's Innate Abilities program, the Twelve Days of Awakening and became certified as an Awakening Coach. I also attended Jennifer's one year intensive, Flight School.

And step-by-dream I shed my logical dependencies—as well as my fears, my tendency to carry others, and my reluctance to set barriers around my time and my energy—and started to "yes" my way through life. I built a successful business. I raised my children to become thriving young adults. I wrote three more books. And I fell in love again. Today I am poised on the crest of a future—a today, even—that I cannot yet imagine. But I know it's full of surprises, and I am enthusiastically available to experience them all. No matter what comes my way, I know I will flourish.

In this book, Jennifer sets out the bridges she invites us all to cross along the path to the thriving way of being in the world she so clearly sees for each of us. She explains the system she encourages her clients to use to awaken to the truth of who we truly are while paradoxically encouraging us to stop using "systems" to get through life. She invites us to Dance with what presents. To play. To say, "Yes!"

As you read this heartfelt foray into the magic of looking at your life from a new direction, Jennifer will help you simultaneously confirm your own brilliance and relinquish the stories that you have been unintentionally using to muffle your own joy. She will share some of the most beautiful aspects of her Operating System for Thriving, for living in a state of Flow that has you continuously upgrading your experiences as you waltz ever more steadily into the embrace of your very own heart.

UNSTUCK is not a woo-woo recipe for drinking a little new-age Kool-Aid, throwing a Band-Aid over our boo-boos and pretending life is all better now. Heck no! It is a grounded manual for living that leverages the ever-evolving sciences of our world to investigate ways of living fuller lives. Jennifer reminds us that life doesn't have to be a complex, shame-laden journey into why we are miserable. It can be an exhilarating rollercoaster ride to personal freedom that whirls us through Fun Island at least as often as it swings us down Compassion Alley.

This book truly is not solely about getting unstuck—from your past, your paradigms, and your preference for predictability. It will encourage you to get comfortable with being uncomfortable so you can fly. And it brings answers to questions you might not even have known your soul was asking.

Jennifer has spent decades becoming the only person on the planet who could write this powerful book. With a background in accounting and economics and years of astutely climbing the corporate ladder, she courageously set it all aside to go on the adventure of finding out how to thrive vibrantly in this multifaceted human experience we share. She has built hugely successful businesses, spoken on stages around the world, and studied with some of the world's most powerful wisdom-keepers. She has seen beyond the veil of this dimension into aspects of the Universe that some of us only dream exist, and although she has never told me this herself, I would not be at all surprised to learn that she has heard the angels sing.

One of the things to be aware of as you read this book is that the wisdom Jennifer shares is likely to be an evolution of what you may have learned from other mentors in this space. She goes quite a few steps farther down the path than those who have gone before, and she has developed some fascinating distinctions that will undoubtedly surprise, delight, and inspire you.

Above all else, I can affirm that Jennifer has dedicated herself to the pursuit of living passionately. She models it in her own life, and she has brought the gift of how to go about doing that to tens of thousands of people.

By the time I had spent a few years rubbing shoulders with Jennifer Hough, Mistress of the Miraculous, I had learned to stop rationalizing everything in life and just lean in. So, when Jennifer asked if I wanted to take her place on a seventeen-day trip to New Zealand with a group of other mission-based entrepreneurs, I was prepared. Participants were to go on some adventure excursions (like bungee jumping and luging down a mountain), give a TED-type talk on stage in a rugby stadium, and spend a week with the aforementioned Waitaha People. My rational mind immediately took control and spit out every reason this was a dumb idea. It was expensive. Some of the activities sounded scary. There was no way I could take that much time away from my business. And how was my family going to manage without me?

A split second later, I said, "Yes!"

And that has made all the difference. The money showed up, the business survived beautifully, and my family had a wonderful chance to practice their domestic survival skills.

And I embarked upon the journey of a lifetime, one that expanded my sense of who I am in the world and gave me even more tools for assisting the people I am here to serve. I met some wonderful people, and I had a whole lot of *fun* on that trip! All because I drew upon an Operating System that I have integrated—some days much better than others—into how I "do" my life.

Jennifer brings a gracious wonder to the puzzle of our humanity, and she does it with brilliance, insight, and compassion. Read this book with an open mind and, more importantly, an open heart. Hear Jennifer's words with an eye on your own inner truth and ask yourself to take whatever bold steps resonate with you as you summon yourself into a new timeline for your life, one where neither the past nor the future can block your ability to thrive, and where your Present Moments entice you into an ever-greater appreciation for the gift that is your Life.

In joy and gratitude,
Susan Crossman
Founder of The Awakening Author
www.awakeningauthor.com

INTRODUCTION

"We are called to be architects of the future, not its victims."
Buckminster Fuller

"What is the most fulfilling thing you can do in the most productive way that would use your unique skills optimally and make a contribution that makes your heart sing, such that you would wake up excited every morning while enjoying your life in ridiculous abundance in every way?"

When my friend first asked me this question years ago, it resonated so deeply with me that my entire life's focus shifted. I was scared but excited for the answer.

Once I answered the question, however, there was no going back. In answering the question, something came unstuck in me that I didn't even know was stuck.

Fast forward ten years, and here we are: witnessing global challenges such as the COVID-19 outbreak, political infighting, social unrest, catastrophic fires, millennial floods, and the polarization now taking place between people, even in the best of families.

I find it troubling that these events coincide with more isolation and less personal contact with people other than our immediate families. We've been forced to be with ourselves more and therefore cannot escape any incongruencies in our lives that have been hiding behind the busyness. This is great because we are in a time that is catalyzing positive change toward what would fulfill our souls, and yet, our little protective identities don't like change.

I have spent an excessive amount of time being introspective, and sometimes it's been uncomfortable. Everything is up for questioning or change for me right now, my relationship to life, my sweetie, my purpose, and my goals.

Statistics show that I am not alone in feeling this way. One-quarter of adults in the US either moved homes or knew someone that moved in 2020. The percentages are higher for people who've changed jobs during that same time frame. People are up-leveling the qualities they want in a home, partner, and career.

It feels like we are in the middle of a massive global reset.[1]

Change is inevitable; even the Universe is constantly evolving. And yet, even before the pandemic and lockdown, some people I know were working hard and trying to "get theirs," hunker down, and save for retirement, seeking control, safety, and predictability. I call this survival.

But we aren't here to merely survive.

We're here to thrive.

An Angel on Earth

It was a harshly cold evening when I first met Angel. I had been working part time with youth on the streets in downtown Toronto. When I met her, Angel was only fifteen years old, a tiny blonde, one hundred pounds soaking wet. She was so pretty, and she looked so young and innocent, a direct contrast to the stark neighborhood we were in.

1 Jaime Ducharme, "Why the COVID-19 Pandemic Has Caused a Widespread Existential Crisis," Time, December 29, 2020, https://time.com/5925218/covid-19-pandemic-life-decisions/.

My supervisor asked me to walk Angel to get a psychiatric evaluation. It was a short walk from one building to another. I was told not to talk to Angel about her issues and to remain neutral and impersonal.

Naturally, I did not follow a single one of those guidelines. Within minutes, I was holding Angel's hand. She was scared. Yet she spoke so coherently of her volatile and painful life with her brothers, who all abused her in various ways. That's why she left her home. We walked and talked for fifteen minutes. When I left her off at the appropriate building, I could feel the weight and precariousness of her situation. She might make it, but likely she would not.

I fell to my knees at the bottom of the steps near a church. I looked up to the sky and asked, "Why would you make the suffering so vivid and personal to me? I have no idea what to do with this!"

Who was I talking to? I was young, still in inquiry about who or what God was. But whoever I was talking to responded.

I felt my answer through the cells of my body, as though I was "seeing" with my cells what there was to do, and then I had to translate the answer into words.

The answer went something like this: "Every person in this world is a piece of the puzzle. Angel played her part. You are here to build bridges for people called by their hearts to make their families, workplaces, and communities a better place. They are the visible and invisible leaders of a new tomorrow, and they won't know it because they will simply be focused on changing their own personal worlds. It is possible to end suffering, but more importantly, it is possible that even kids like Angel and her unhealed, overwhelmed parents can thrive. Your job is to figure out the operating system to thrive and then teach as many people as you can to embody that way of being. It is your natural state. Any *one* person living in their own heavenly flow would never take power away from another, and even more wonderfully, would activate that same possibility in those around them. Any person living in the presence of Infinite Wisdom would only want to create a life that was inspired and creative on the path to being fulfilled while living out their greatest life of contribution and meaning. First, you must embody it yourself to teach it."

Angel revealed that I could feel how sensitive I was to incongruencies in the world. I decided then and there that I would not live a life that solely "survived" this world. I decided to find out how to use the contrast not to depress me, but to fuel my passionate, relentless pursuit of uncovering the Thriving Operating System. I was determined to live the most fulfilling life and make the greatest contribution I could while most productively creating and enjoying every drop of meaning and abundance with which I would be blessed...*and then pay it forward* to those that want to live the same way.

This book is part of doing exactly that.

Are You Fully Here?

Over the past twenty years, I've helped people answer questions like the one I shared at the beginning of this introduction in a unique and transformational way so they can live out their best lives as the best version of themselves. But first, they have to willingly get unstuck from humanity's paradigms, the destructive underlying beliefs based on "shoulds," "musts," and "have-tos" that restrict so many of us from becoming all we're capable of. The Wide Awakening (TWA) is the company I developed to transcend that stuckness.

Our lives are meant to be lived as our unique expression, not according to a government, theology, guru, or some expert saying what's best for *them*. We are meant to thrive, living our lives intentionally on purpose, in meaning, with intimacy, so much so that we're super excited to get up in the morning.

It's even possible to live that way during a time of great polarity.

Nothing will change until millions of us live congruently with our heart's calling, which will light the way for the rest of humanity. We can't wait for circumstances to change; we must facilitate the change. We are what we seek.

Ask yourself this question: "Am I choosing to fully be here, alive, in my glory, on this planet?" Just by asking the question, you start to change your neurochemistry.

You're telling your cells that you are interested in living, not just a little, but a lot, that your life matters. What would it look like for you to fully choose to thrive in your life without hedging your bets because of the trouble in the world?

Go on, take a moment to ask yourself if you fully choose to be here.

At The Wide Awakening (TWA), our clients are asked to participate in an intake study to gauge their progress. Past clients have told us that, on average, they are consciously choosing to be here in their lives 62 percent of the time. This means that life is only returning 62 percent to them. Life responds to the exact degree to which you lean in.

Some people will never ask themselves these questions. Some will but won't admit that they haven't fully leaned into their life because they don't want to sound ungrateful for what they already have or feel overwhelmed by the change they know is coming.

This is why I'm writing this book. This is why I want you to know about this work.

In subsequent chapters, I'm going to show you the way to answer those questions, implement the answers, and embody a new way of being that makes you feel more fulfilled. Instead of being a victim of what is going on out there, you become a shining beacon of what is possible.

You may read the book from start to finish in order of chapter or choose to open to whatever chapter feels resonant after reading chapters one and two to give you context. Each chapter will take you deeper into the concept being *UNSTUCK*, yet this book is not written in a progression. No matter where you open the book, you'll be in the right place.

Your friends and family are also looking for someone to show them what's possible. You can be that person, not by what you say but by how you live your most fulfilling life. This book will help you become that person.

> *"There are fractal codes containing the laws of creation, and the more we understand these laws, the more we can apply the harmony that is apparent in nature as a more powerful force in our own lives. There is truth and purity in natural things, and our contact with them nourishes the soul and illuminates the mind."*
> Jonathan Quintin

From Shaman to Science

Eighteen years ago, I fell seriously ill. During that time, through a series of wakened dreams, I was shown by my guides and angels that our evolution as humans has led us to have the capacity for living a fulfilled life and that doing so is about awakening to the deeper truths of who we are and why we are here. When you start to live a life of meaning, you change your relationship to the past, retroactively transmuting hundreds of old patterns, beliefs, and thoughts.

Because of experiences like those dreams, along with the awareness I received after witnessing Angel's suffering, I became hardwired to seek new tools to continually facilitate our work.

My journey of developing the system and tools for living *UNSTUCK* and thriving forward in life started over twenty years ago, as I began working with mystics, physicists, biologists, neuroscientists, sociologists, shamans, religious leaders, spiritual teachers, business leaders, and thought leaders worldwide. Teachings from all of these fields and more make up the foundational wisdom that underlies *UNSTUCK*. Our clients tell us that our systems and techniques have helped them effectively navigate change and polarity with grace through living a life that follows our natural flow.

I continue to do my own work constantly to embody, evolve, and play with that Thriving Operating System and pay it forward. This book is the result of what Angel gave me that day that brought me to my knees on the church step—she gave me the opportunity to come to the threshold of the doorway to help us transcend the pain of the past on the fast track. She truly was an angel.

The programs I created through The Wide Awakening, such as Get Out of Your Own Way™ and The Thriving Operating System, have now been taught in three languages in over fifteen countries. Without knowing it, that beautiful earth angel catalyzed me to my purpose, in perfect timing, in the perfect way.

In the next several chapters, you'll discover that The Wide Awakening approach to transformation is revolutionary. Becoming all you came here to be does not involve excavating your past, analyzing cause and effect, or mirroring back to you who other people see when they look at you. We don't go looking for what is broken. You are not broken, and you don't need fixing.

This book is for you. At The Wide Awakening, we're about the fast track, and that means becoming more of who you really are, so there's little room left for anything or anyone else. The tools I've developed are designed to transcend and transmute the old patterns of being so you can embody a new way of being.

The clients who chose me to illuminate the path forward are the ones who deserve celebrating. They're the real heroes of this story, casting off years, lifetimes in some cases, of conditioning, judgment, and doubt to discover who they really are.

They took a leap of faith and allowed their heart's calling to speak more loudly than their protective identities. That kind of commitment is sacred to me. It involves following the subtle whispers of our hearts, whispers that emerge out of the cracks of least resistance.

You've heard them too, haven't you? Do you hear the subtle whisper inside, even if you've never admitted to anyone else, that says something else is possible for your life and this world?

Listen to Your Heart

A famous teacher of success principles came to see me. He was having a total breakdown because his multimillion-dollar business was no longer working.

He told me, "People are changing during these times, and I know that my work has evolved as well, but for some reason, I no longer know how to articulate what I feel."

We started with *UNSTUCK* and proceeded through The Wide Awakening systems. His company's direction completely shifted within a year, and he conquered a persistent addiction. He successfully realigned his entire life to realize his greatest path of contribution.

He had to let go of everything he thought he knew, which he did with grace. He now has clients from all over the world and has written two books in the last two years. He has answered those life-changing questions for himself, expanding spiritually and putting real-life systems in place to enjoy the synergy that comes from truly being and doing what he was born for.

We can no longer settle for "good enough." This kind of call for a better life is palpable. It is cellular. If you look, you will feel it calling you. It's time for divine intolerance. That is to say, intolerance to that which does not match the reason we were born or the evolution that is calling us forward toward a life that feeds our souls.

Just look at what is happening in the world due to our inattention.

As you'll read, there is a difference between logically collecting evidence for a life that is "good enough" and living your life according to the call of your heart's desire.

In times of great change, the call can be strong or subtle depending on how steeped we are in our current way of being, our stubbornness, and how much dissonance we are experiencing between what is and what we know can be. My experience has been that the longer I waited, the bigger the leap I had to make. Leaps that I waited much longer than I needed to were both inevitable and uncomfortable.

The Fast Track

Our old ways of awakening are no longer aligned with the speed at which we are being asked to embody ourselves. The time for living in a karmic reality, finding a guru, or giving our power away is over. We are our own gurus.

Our powerful desires for more meaning and depth are causing us to find new ways to evolve so we can keep up with the speed of the answers waiting for us. Those desires ask us to learn, understand, and adopt an operating system that allows us to flourish and feel connected to life in a new way that aligns with our true nature.

In realizing who you are and what you are capable of, you become a person that transforms and transmutes the very events that originally hurt you. That is true freedom. It's also how the world changes in quantum leaps and bounds.

I have almost died five times in my life, and each time I have been aware of how precious this life and this world are. I have had to transcend the need to carry the world, and people I love, the hard way.

I started writing this book kicking and screaming despite the catalyst of change in the air that was begging me to get it done. It's a big shift for me to leave the safety bubble of my clients and team for the greater world. I want to be transparent and vulnerable with you because if we can't be vulnerable with each other, nothing will ever change.

I was inspired to write this book in response to the chaos that a lot of people are feeling. So many of you are stuck, just like I was before that powerful question helped me get unstuck and thriving forward in life.

One of the reasons I created The Wide Awakening was to help clients remake their lives with the emphasis on deeper fulfillment and meaning.

The adventure continues, and isn't it great that we can use someone else's expertise to improve our journey without needing to do the heavy lifting?

I am excited to share my expertise and experience, acknowledging that I stand on the shoulders of those who have come before me.

Thank you for being courageous enough to have gotten this far in your life and have enough curiosity to go on the adventure of your heart's calling.

I invite you to read this book with a healthy sense of curiosity. If you do, there is a very good chance you will find exactly what you need to live out your heart's calling. You will find that the concepts here will make your awakening, fulfillment, and evolution much simpler.

If life is calling you, are you going to pick up?

I have.

Remember one important fact: **you are not broken and don't need fixing**. Please read this book from that vantage point. That shift in perspective alone will enable you to embody the information deeply.

I look forward to meeting you on the playing field, in our groups and programs, and out in life.

Game on.

You aren't alone. There is always a way to become *UNSTUCK.*

XOXOXO,

Jennifer

CHAPTER 1

BRAIN BRIDGES SO YOU CAN BE²

*"No problem can be solved from the same
level of consciousness that created it."*
Albert Einstein

When I was experiencing the series of wakened dreams that I mentioned in the introduction, one of the dreams answered a question that had been stumping me.

The question was this: "Why do we have to shift one belief at a time, or a couple at a time? If a bunch of thoughts that we think over and over become beliefs (after collecting evidence for the rightness of thoughts), and a bunch of beliefs when married together become an entirely personal or cultural paradigm, then why don't we shift perspectives on the whole paradigm instead of just the beliefs?" To give you an example, when I first started as a Nutritionist (I used to run the largest practice in Canada), I just gave people direct health advice. Change what you eat, and your body will change. What I found out was that the changes didn't last. So I asked why? That's when I started to understand that patterns of thought create your biochemistry and if you don't change those patterns, the weight will come back because your body, and life for that matter, will default to match your beliefs. Then I realized that there are patterns of beliefs too. In the case of weight loss for instance, there is a whole pattern of beliefs from your family, so even if we change one belief about your body, that will get overridden by your familial paradigm. A familial paradigm might sound like this:

"Our family has slow metabolism, and we like to eat. We are big boned. Stressing and carrying people is just how the women in my family are. We eat our emotions." It was then that I realized, if I can change the whole paradigm, all of the beliefs would follow. I knew that this shift in the way we shift was the key why the work we do at TWA is so different.

I hadn't heard anyone ever answer that question, but I was shown the answer in the wakened dreams: "You can shift entire paradigms and therefore hundreds of beliefs at a time."

I was shown that there aren't many people shifting entire paradigms at once in a way that changes our body's biochemistry and level of attraction, and I was told: "Have fun creating that technique." This is the origin of Brain Bridges. Yes, I am so grateful for my Divine Impatience that wasn't satisfied with the flow of my journey to meaning and fulfillment.

These Brain Bridges are the bridges of understanding that allow your left brain—the logical, analytical brain—to loosen its grip on the beliefs keeping you stuck in the never-ending cycle of survival. Building these bridges is necessary to fully experience the shifts available in the activations throughout this book.

The best way for me to explain a Brain Bridge is this: a part of your brain wants to protect you from past pains, and over time if you collect enough evidence for the pain happening, you will develop neurological highways that become hardwired.

There is also a part of your brain that deals with possibility and creativity and tells you that you are unstoppable. (There is a great TED Talk on the subject of the right and left brain on our Resources page at https://thewideawakening.com/unstuck-resources.) Based on our experience with tens of thousands of clients, connecting to the land of pure possibility and creative solutions is possible. This can happen through learning how to have your right brain build a bridge to your left brain and convince it that a thought, belief, or paradigm doesn't make sense anymore. If it no longer makes sense, then the thought, belief, or paradigm is held more loosely. This makes the brain much more receptive to building a new, more expansive neuropathway that matches your new, more freeing awareness.

The intention of this chapter is to show you Brain Bridges in action while deepening these three things:

- Your resolve to know that flourishing is possible for you
- Your passion for learning how to thrive
- Your understanding of the scientific information that supports thriving so your mind can be at peace and receptive

Brain Bridges

I have developed the Brain Bridges tool over time while working with clients. This tool has allowed me to help my clients, my team, and myself shift hundreds of beliefs at a time. The paradox is that we are not directly addressing stuck or suboptimal beliefs to do that. We are doing that by transforming entire paradigms using an understanding of how physics, the cosmos, and our biology work, and that in turn shifts multiple beliefs at a time.

Here's an example of a paradigm shift through building a Brain Bridge that broke hundreds of beliefs for one of my clients, Rob.

Rob came into our Get Out of Your Own Way™ program with his arms folded and a big ole scowl on his face. When I asked Rob how he found us, he replied curtly, "My wife drove me here. She made me come."

My only thought was, "Uh oh. One of *those*."

Rob had arrived early and started complaining about the temperature in the room, wondering aloud if we could afford to heat. Oh boy.

After the rest of the participants joined us and we began, I asked Rob once more, "What is *your* reason for being here, regardless of what your wife may have said?"

Rob hadn't even considered what his own answer might be. It was, however, becoming clear to me that it was very brave of him to come and that he must actually love his wife very much. The look on his face, however, screamed, "I came to shut my wife up."

But what came out of his mouth was different from that.

Rob said, "I suppose that I am probably really hard to live with." No shit.

I said, "Thanks for being so vulnerable, Rob. Let's just dive in while we are having a good chat."

Usually, I would have started the program with a whole bunch of stage setting and context. But this time, I knew it was right to dive in.

I then asked Rob a series of questions like: Where did you grow up? How many siblings did you have? And what is the most stressful event you remember from your childhood?

I discovered that Rob had endured one of the most dysfunctional childhoods I had ever heard about. He and his siblings lived in abject fear, as their mother was unpredictably volatile. Often, when he was six, seven, and eight, she would wield a knife. Rob shared a story about one time in particular when his mother threw the knife at him with the obvious intent to kill him.

There were some wide eyes and gasps in the room as he shared this, given that we had just met Rob. At the same time, his classmates were leaning in with compassion.

He shared with me that when he was little, all he ever wanted was someone to see him, talk to him, nurture him, give him praise, have his back. That was his single prayer. He wanted a true feeling of family.

I told him how sorry I was that he experienced that. He cried, as did I.

I asked Rob about his life now. He told me that he had great friends who put up with him, saw him, supported him through tough times, and loved him unconditionally. They visited him at work and came for dinner, and they did fun things together. He got teary again describing his friends, but this time in a good way.

Then I spoke my first Brain Bridge. I had never spoken these words before; they just came through me. But these words built a bridge between Rob's heart's knowingness and his messy and unproductive perspective on his family.

I said, "Dear Rob, God, the Universe, All that Is, Creation knew exactly who your family would be before you got here and that most of them would not be related to you."

Silence.

Then, tears from everyone.

Those few words shifted Rob's entire paradigm about family. He dropped his expectation that his mother should be different. He realized that he had created the family he wanted as a direct result of the family he didn't have. He even said that his "soul family" was far more delicious than most people's biological families. He was also able to see that the entire Universe is what birthed him and parented him through those trying times, Unconditionally, relentlessly loving him and guiding him to stay alive. And we realized together that our true parent is Creation, which is where we get the silly expectation that fallible humans should be as perfect as Creation is. To make the point again, all of his beliefs changed about family at once because we shifted the paradigm of family.

This is what we will do throughout the rest of the book. We will find the deeper truths about paradigms that relate to important parts of your life. If you lean in, you will be able to transcend hundreds of beliefs with every couple of chapters.

For me, being able to shift paradigms so that the whole constellation of associated beliefs can then realign is a super juicy result.

The Idea of Being One

Much like Rob in the story above, we spend time and emotional energy (even lifetimes) trying to belong to our families, cultures, or workplaces. We morph ourselves to fit in. It's painful, for good reason. Because we were born with unique skills, trajectories, personalities, gifts, and reasons for being alive. You were given feelings to let you know when you are not being who you came here to be. You feel contractive when you don't match your expansive nature. Hence, you were not born to fit in with anyone else. The Universe already dreamed your perfection into this life. Acceptance by the Universe is assumed. Curiosity on the adventure is what it takes, rather than safety in sameness.

Oneness is best described by Rumi (man, I love this dude): "Out beyond ideas of wrongdoing and right-doing, there is a field. I'll meet you there."

This quote also represents the description of a Brain Bridge. When we struggle with getting it right, Life responds to that request. Life's response is always informed by greater wisdom, and that response lies in the field. These days, with all that is going on, there is definitely a calling to return to that field where the answers that serve all of humanity lie.

In a Survival Operating System, the goal is to belong in society and with each other. This is about acceptance, approval, being enough, validation, and lovability by other fallible humans. Survival always offers us solutions that feel contractive instead of expansive.

In fact, we are so supported by Life that we have those built-in feelings to let us know if we are contracting or expanding energetically (regardless of emotional feeling, because sometimes what is in front of us seems scary to our personality).

What feels more expansive to you? That we are here to work hard at fitting in and that one day if we try hard enough at changing ourselves for others, it will all just come together and we will be fulfilled? Or that we are unique expressions of Infinite Wisdom/Creation/God/Existence and that we are already unconditionally loved by that same Infinite Wisdom? In fact, by engaging our superpowers and our ever-evolving personality and toolbox through the trajectory we've been sent on, the Universe gets information through a feedback loop and expands in its own awareness. The actions taken in resonance with your purpose cause an expansive feeling because you are aligned with the exact potentials that the Universe sees for you.

That feeling of expansiveness is your validation that you are in flow. That alignment gets translated through our body as woo-hoo! or yes! or goosebumps or fun. That is the feeling of you and greater wisdom being excited that you are acting and thinking in the general direction of your highest and best life. That is the feeling of creating upon creation using your skills and your personality in the most aligned way.

Based on Nassim Haramein's work, we've learned that our atoms actually contain the entire universe and everything that has ever existed, including the history of how we got there. (For more on Nassim Haramein's work, visit the Resources page at https://thewideawakening.com/unstuckresources.) Our atoms, therefore, contain the knowledge of our lives and who we are. New science demonstrates that photons communicate between two people's trillions of cells and therefore bodies, at the speed of light which travels around the world seven times in a second. The speed of sound is much slower of course, using our one voice and two ears. I like to think of this cellular communication as "see feel hearing".[2] We have around 37 trillion cells, all communing with those around us.[3] Plants do the same. This is happening all day, every day.

My point is that our deep connection to each other in "the field" is assumed by the Universe; it is not something we are trying to get back to. It just is. It's part of our mechanics. The true point of realizing how connected we all are and that we all have access to the same tools to flourish while being individual

2 Emily Conover, "Two-Way Communication Is Possible with a Single Quantum Particle," Science News, February 2018, https://www.sciencenews.org/article/two-way-communication-possible-single-quantum-particle.

3 Ananda L. Roy and Richard S. Conroy, "Toward Mapping the Human Body at a Cellular Resolution," Molecular Biology of the Cell 29, number 15 (August 2018): 1779–1785, https://www.ncbi.nlm.nih.gov/pmc/articles/PMC6085824/.

and unique expressions of the whole leads me to ask: What can we do with this Ferrari (this Essence in a body)? What can we do since we have access to the resources of "all that is"? How many Superpowers do I not even know about? And what can we cocreate, given all of that information?

For me, it's not that interesting to return to being "one" with each other. We already are "one" in the Universe. It's more about what we can do individually and together now that we know we have access to Life.

As above could really be "so below," in the truest, most scientific sense. In other words, the recognition that our "oneness" is assumed at a macro Universal level and a micro fractal level should have us very curious about what's possible on a three dimensional level as individual humans.

And what is the point of having access to all of the wisdom that has ever been if you can't hear it, tune in to it, or make sense of it? There isn't a point.

This is why it's vital we build Brain Bridges, which are all about accessing infinite wisdom by first acknowledging that the minute we struggle is the minute there is an answer and then getting out of the way of it.

Brain Bridges Rock

Let's talk briefly about this paradigm/belief thing for a moment.

This is pretty crucial, as the next twelve chapters rely on you understanding how Brain Bridges provide a revolution in the way we evolve. The effect will be long-lasting, subtle at first, and often leave you feeling unfamiliar. That's a good sign that you are shifting.

Before I developed Brain Bridges, changing my life at the level of thought was just way too slow for me, and I love efficiency. For me, using affirmations, repetition, and "cancel/ clear" were all just more arduous than they needed to be. According to the National Science Foundation, an average person has about 12,000 to 60,000 thoughts per day. Keep that in mind as we talk about beliefs.

If you think certain thoughts for long enough, you start collecting evidence for those thoughts. This evidence becomes beliefs, like "I'm really uncoordinated," "I'm terrible with money," or "based on my family experience, love hurts." Eventually, if you collect enough evidence for these thoughts, you will believe them to be accurate, and your actions will reflect your beliefs. You won't play certain sports; you might spend money without thought or concern, and your muscles might brace every time you walk into your family home. Beliefs affect the way you plug into and navigate life.

Now allow me to show you where my brain went with this concept. Let's say you have over three hundred sets of beliefs (about aging, your health, genetics, money, love, men, women, and so on). Most of these came from conditioning from your past, ancestry, parents, school, socioeconomic lot in life, race/ ethnicity, religion, etc. And all of those beliefs were just originally a collection of thoughts.

Most people, of course, think that their beliefs are true and try to enroll others or even fight with others about those beliefs. That's how wars start.

What if we could make quantum leaps in freeing ourselves from unproductive beliefs? That question led me to explore the possibility of upgrading an entire paradigm. A paradigm is when you take a group of beliefs and lump them together to create a certain environment where everyone holds the same beliefs in common. We have paradigms about marriage, family, raising children, politics, economics, how to manage your health, and so on.

Remember I told you that I am the efficiency queen? And, although I have recovered from perfectionism, I used to be a *huge* Type A personality. Combine those two characteristics, and you get someone who tenaciously pursued a new paradigm for evolving our ability to awaken and thrive. I got super-duper tired of analyzing all of my beliefs.

I also knew I didn't want to address my thoughts to affect positive change in my life because that was too slow. I still desired my thoughts to change, however. So, I did lots of work initially to address changing my beliefs, which, of course, would naturally affect my thoughts. At some point, however, I realized that if beliefs were just over-thunk thoughts, I needed a paradigm shift about how to thrive.

The end results we are seeking are transcendence from confining paradigms and the ability to hold all of our beliefs loosely. It isn't about eliminating beliefs, which is deeply difficult to do, given that thoughts and therefore beliefs are wired into the brain, although those can and will change over time. A paradigm we have held to is that you need to eliminate unconstructive beliefs before you can thrive or get unstuck. Not true, and yet so many people wait for that release, which would keep people unnecessarily working on old patterns for years and never getting on with their lives.

Not believing your beliefs may already be happening in this discussion, so already, you might be open to holding your beliefs loosely while you get curious about the new reality that you can build. At one point, the world was thought to be flat, butter was bad, and smoking was good. Holding strongly to beliefs is another way that our personality can feel safe. But you are never safer than when you are going direct with Life's wisdom, without filters, and creating new realities that allow you to alchemically influence your world without being restricted by protective beliefs.

Here's an example: if I had addressed the migraines I used to experience from the beliefs associated with the paradigm of a medical doctor, I would have been on medication the rest of my life. Fortunately, medicine didn't work in my case, *and* I am super tenacious. I came at the migraines from the paradigm of epigenetics instead, which offers the science that shows that our bodies are directly influenced by what we think and how we look at life. The migraines went away the instant I realized they came from a well-practiced thought habit of pressure that I put on myself, which went all the way back into my dad's lineage. The pressure wasn't even mine…it was from a bunch of men from my past that I didn't even know. I had to change the paradigm through which I saw all health issues to access answers not available medically.

There are lots of people helping others change their perspectives on beliefs. It's great. Every revolution in our ability to evolve is fantastic. One day this body of work will be a building block for something else as well. Consider that it is a new paradigm to talk about changing perspectives on a paradigm rather than beliefs.

As you read, it is essential to experience the next twelve Brain Bridges (in the next twelve chapters) from that perspective.

Here are some notes that I made when I first received awakened dreams describing how life ought to be working for us.

Brain Bridges and the Laws of Thriving

A client of mine was particularly frustrated with her progress in her life. "Why does it take so long to get to thriving?" she asked.

I had a pat answer prepared, but instead of giving her that, I decided to write down the Laws of Thriving that I had learned in my first few years of teaching. I asked this client to pay close attention to the first two laws.

Here are the Five Laws of Thriving.

The First Law of Thriving

We weren't meant to fix ourselves because
we've never been broken.

It's like having a ladder tall enough to get to Heaven, yet putting it up against the building to Hell. It's like you've received all the tools to flourish, but because you analyze and judge yourself, life keeps delivering you more things to fix, and so round and round we go. We were meant to learn the skills, paradigm shifts, and operating system for thriving and then embody them. Spending our precious life remembering our natural state causes us to see our so-called brokenness from a higher perspective, whereby we start to care less about what we perceive has been stopping us. Having that higher perspective causes us to be able to transmute hundreds of beliefs that keep us stuck at a time. We are no longer scared because we can see how to thrive.

The idea that we need fixing has been in the fabric of society for a while. For example, consider how people approach the Law of Attraction. Many people approach LOA with the perspective that they are doing something wrong if things don't manifest—as though how they are approaching it is the problem.

The truth is LOA (at least, the original personal development version of it) is not the issue. Your entire life, every waking hour, is a function of magnetics. We are walking, breathing magnets to where we put our attention and the paradigms running in the background. The issue is that we want to feel safe and feel in control of life, so we ask for things in our minds through intention that we think would fix our lives. LOA never facilitates manifestations through the perspective of that mistruth—that we are broken. So, when you try to manifest something out of fixing your finances, your house, your relationship, or your health out of the frustration that it is broken, Life cannot deliver through that perspective. It's inconsistent with the Universal truth that you are here to Create in perfection as a Creator. If you are here to Create in every way on any subject, nothing will ever be in its finished form, or what the heck would we create? There is always more. In other words, from a certain perspective, everything is broken or forever unfinished.

That means there is and was never anything to fix, only things to create upon.

So be aware. The spirit in which you experience this book, live your life, go to a massage therapist, eat your food is everything. Excitedly anticipating the unimagined in a way that tickles your telomeres (at the end of your chromosomes) as you lean into what's before you while acting on what life brings you gets you very different results than saying, "Fix me, I'm broken. Once I'm fixed, then I can thrive."

Law of Attraction (LOA) in our world means that you are always attracting, and intention is just something to keep your mind busy while the Universe delivers anyhow.

When using LOA, many people ask, "How do you manipulate life to get what you want?" That's survival-based thinking. Most of them are asking for what would make them feel safe and in control or fix their lives.

In thriving, however, the most productive question to ask of LOA is: "How do I stay connected in flow enough to live out the inevitable miraculous nature of my life knowing full well that the basis for life is magnetic and that all things are coming to me whether I mentally intend or not? I am a walking intention, and Life has access to resources that would deliver to me that which I could never imagine or intend. So how can I stay aligned with that frequency of all that goodness and simply be surprised and delighted by what manifests in my life?"

The Second Law of Thriving

When you focus on a subject, whether good or
bad, physics responds. If you think something
is important enough to evaluate, analyze or
think on, Life does not argue with you. It
will give you more opportunity to experience
similar circumstances.

Figuring out why stuff happens can bring mental peace but leaves us with two results that are suboptimal. First, given the laws of physics that say what you give attention to is what expands, you are telling Life that you are interested in analyzing more examples of stuckness. Second, while you are spending your precious energy dollars on analysis, you are not learning how to thrive. Often, analysis can calm the mind so that you can access deeper truths that will displace the old unproductive patterns, but ultimately having confidence in your ability to thrive makes those unproductive patterns far less interesting.

The Third Law of Thriving

You truly were born to be your own guru.

Nobody else is pouring through your body but you. As I'll talk about in a later chapter, information comes to you through your cells and your emotional filters; it is exactly designed for you and not someone else. That is not to say that there aren't great guides out there that can pick up on your information—because there are. But you get to run anything that anyone says through your own cells to see if it feels right in your heart or not.

The Fourth Law of Thriving

You don't need to eliminate an unproductive pattern to have it stop governing your life. You only need to make it less interesting.

Most people wait to eliminate the old before flying forward. In our work, we make the old stuckness way less interesting first. That's part of how we can shift hundreds of beliefs at a time. You help people first to know who they are before you excavate who they are not. It's ingenious.

The Fifth Law of Thriving

You are a living intention, embodied from the
day you were born.

This will always override any mental intention. As long as you are taking action forward in one way or another, you will either be affirmed or redirected by life. You are a magnet to people, places, and circumstances that fulfill the intention that you are, not the intention that you make.

The issue is almost always the frequency/vibration/level of the emotions that we are tuned in to. There is more waiting for us than we could ever receive in one lifetime, already, right now. It is a benevolent Universe that is wired to make sure everything happens for us and not to us. It isn't a question of getting out of your way; it's a question of lining up with the Universe's way, exactly as nature operates, as it happens.

The five laws above became the basis for the first program in fast-tracking our clients to live in fulfillment and fun in life called Get Out of Your Own Way™. It has changed so much for so many clients in the past fifteen years. In the chapters to come, you will experience some of the leading-edge techniques that we use in Get Out of Your Own Way™. These five laws work in unison to bring lasting results that are not just expected but even better than expected. We call these results 'or betters.'

Here is a little about the 'or betters' that happen when you up your game to thriving.

Or Betters

'Or betters' are what happen when we relinquish the need to intend. Stay with me on this. 'Or betters' are prevalent when we simply remember ourselves as the embodied intention of everything we've ever lived in any life. 'Or betters' happen when we remember we have free will to choose, assuming all the while that trajectory is the result of every past life, every desire, and every prayer you have ever prayed. 'Or betters' happen when you live like control is overrated. They happen when you understand that the resources of Creation, omnipotent and omniscient as it is, will deliver you something so far beyond what your lovely (please don't hate me) pea brain can come up with as an intention. Your brain only accesses your history, TV shows, and what you got taught in school, and who wants to live out that history again? Your greater Wisdom is constantly dancing with the trajectory you are on. You are a living intention without ever needing to use your brain to intend. Infinite Wisdom is in a dance with you, responding to your every thought, and action (even moreso), however, it is responding most attentively to your life's purpose. You can't mentally intend your way to an awesome life. Life is responding to that intention that you are, which will override any intention that you make mentally.

All of the solutions that Life will send you will be relentlessly consistent with the futures that are dreaming you.

Your life sent you on a series of possible trajectories that offer you the opportunity to live in a ridiculously awesome way. Those 'or betters' will always override any intention you make to be safe and in control or have a predictable future.

How many of your intentions did you create in order to be safe and in control or have a predictable future?

Next time you do a vision board, make the top one-third of the vision board pictures and words that you come up with. In the other two-thirds, write in big, bold marker 'OR BETTER!'

I realized at one point in my twenties that I was breaking up every relationship I was in. I was also trying to fix every guy I was with so that I could feel safe. Hmmm. Nothing was working. And the only common denominator in the equation was me. Instead of running around agreeing with other women about men being the problem or thinking that I was doomed to a life of loneliness, I decided to play a game to just enjoy the male gender, just for the sake of having fun. I had grown up with all sisters and realized I didn't really understand the world of men (LOL).

My beingness at the time was all about letting love win. It is part of my essence, superseding all other mental intentions. I came in that way. Hence, what manifested in my life in this story was a total 'or better.'

In the process of doing the dating experiment where I went out, platonically, with thirty different dudes in thirty days, something interesting happened.

I lived on my sailboat at the time. And every night, I would go out, and this forty-three-year-old man noticed me every night from the cockpit of his boat (I was thirty at the time). I didn't know that he was noticing me. One night he asked me what I was doing. And I told him that I was playing a dating game.

Or better number 1: We chatted, and at some point, I told him about my Dream List. He listened, and the next day I woke up to a bottle of champagne in my cockpit with an invitation attached and glasses. He took me out on a date that accomplished Dream number 39, hot-air ballooning. Fun. But I was not going to get serious with him because it wasn't part of the game. And he hired me for a big job for his company based on my business consulting experience.

Or better number 2: The check from that consulting gig was the exact amount of my payables. I got out of debt because I decided to focus forward on something that moved energy rather than fixing my problem.

I could never have intended either of those results. It was effortless and even better than what my tiny pea brain would have imagined. Yay!

That's what we are aiming for in the chapters to come, for you and the world in general, frankly. This is all part of my diabolical plot for world peace.

What Does the Science Say?

Here are some of the scientific principles that our work is based on and why we can shift entire paradigms versus one belief at a time.

The laws of physics imply that what you make important to you through your actions, words, and deeds will continue to show itself in your life. Suppose the paradigm in which you are living your entire life is based on a flawed or incongruent fear-based collection of beliefs, or a paradigm. In that case, it will influence every event, person, thought, and interaction that you encounter. You walk around with that perspective in your DNA. Consciousness loves you; you are an ocean in the drop of consciousness (thank you, Rumi). Thoughts are simply the result of the beliefs you hold, which ultimately reflect the paradigms that you live by. If you understand the paradigm of how life works more deeply from a science-based practical approach and can have it make sense to your logical brain, you won't be able to entertain beliefs or thoughts that support your life of struggle.

It's a frustrating time to be alive if you look at the polarity in our lives, much of which currently is being caused by the polarity in the world. *We* don't feel very together. In not feeling together, it can start to feel a bit hopeless.

One important scientific principle of shifting our lives, and therefore the world, is spin and fractals.

We Spin and Physics

The spin of things is a principle that will take an understanding of renowned physicist Nassim Haramein's current thesis. It's also going to take some understanding of the idea of fractals and the holographic Universe. We will unpack that below.

We are one at some level of existence. Scientifically explaining the basis for this paradigm makes it a much more compelling concept. The meaning I found through the scientific explanation was life-changing for me; I hope it is for you as well.

Let's start with some fun facts.

If you were standing completely still, no matter how much you try, you would still be moving. Everything in the Universe is constantly expanding on itself, changing, moving, and spiraling. Consider these facts:

- You are spinning, even when you are standing still, internally biologically, externally in your energy field, and cosmologically.
- So, how fast are you moving right now? The Earth itself moves at a rate of 1,000 miles per hour through our solar

system in a spiral. The solar system moves at a rate of 448,000 miles per hour through our galaxy, and our Milky Way moves at a rate of 1.3 million miles per hour through the cosmos.

- You are immersed in an environment that is always moving and, as a result, is constantly creating upon itself. That affects you, whether you like it or not. You are swimming in a soup of change; the environment for expanding forward in abundance is part of your subatomic structure. It's part of the subatomic structure of anything in 3D.

There is an interesting concept related to gyroscopes (which spin) called precession. In aviation, it means this: The tilting or turning of the rotor axis as a result of some external force. When a deflective force is applied to a gyro rotor that is standing still, the rotor will move in the direction of that force. This movement places the rotor in a new parallel plane of rotation. It is a concept I love because I like gyroscopes and because we all spin. Here's how I interpret this concept of precession: when we are close to each other, imagine that we create precession in consciousness—a parallel possibility or idea. And imagine that is the natural way we are with each other. We are in a constant state of creating something new, at right angles to what exists, and if we pay attention, we can actually live a life filled with the joy of realizing "the new" all the time, instead of trying to make sure that our spirals don't touch. It is foundational to nature and the way we operate.

It is in our DNA to spin. Gosh, our DNA is a spiral. We are not meant to go around in circles on the same plane. Spirals have outward or forward motion. It's in our design on both the meta scale and sub-atomic scale.

The Holographic Universe

Here is the case for the idea that Life is available to you at any time and that if you can shift a paradigm such that you are freer, you not only affect your body, but you affect everyone and everything.

You'll need to know about Einstein and the groundbreaking physicist Nassim Haramein again. Einstein died with all the right ingredients to mathematically explain the Universe at his fingertips, but ironically, he did not have enough time to complete the thesis. A unified field equation is what he was seeking. Many have picked up where he left off. I am sure Einstein is whispering in all of their ears. Haramein picked up where Einstein left off. Using modern tools that Einstein did not have, Haramein figured out how to make the Unified Field Equation balance. We don't have to break it all down for you here, as it's complicated and I am not a physicist—although to hear Haramein explain it is incredibly elegant, as most truths are. And yes, modern physics will have to make a big leap to allow itself to evolve at the level of Haramein's work. But as George Bernard Shaw said, "All great truths start as the biggest (apparent) blasphemies."

The bottom line is that to make his equation work, according to Haramein, the information of the entire universe would have to be available in every proton of every nucleus of every atom. It would have to be an entirely holographic Universe, where any one fractal of consciousness would contain the whole of consciousness. Kind of like your tongue can tell you in Traditional Chinese Medicine everything about your glands and organs, as can your eyes, hands, and feet using reflexology points. Ancient wisdom has been teaching us this principle for eons. I cannot emphasize enough, as Rumi said: "You are not a drop in the ocean; you are the entire ocean in a drop." One of my favorite philosophers and I hope he becomes one of yours too.

I would say that both are true in a holographic Universe. In other words, we contain the stardust that first created worlds, and the wisdom and information of that entire evolution that got us to where we are now is contained in our every atom.

Imagine living knowing that everything that's ever been thought or created, and the process to get there, is within every cell. I mean it. Right now, just pause and imagine yourself living by going directly with the wisdom that is already latent around you, through you, in you, and for you. Wouldn't that make life way more fluid?

Go listen to Haramein's TED Talk if you want more.[4] It's brilliant. You'll also find the link on our resource guide, here https://thewideawakening.com/unstuckresources.

For years now, I have worked with all of my physicist and biologist friends on an abundance of clients and myself, and I have been changing the way I see. I have been seeing the world, my life, the lives of clients, politics, companies, and everything holographically. I can see into future potentials and past incongruencies that give us the present moment, which allows me to help people, companies, and organizations to realign with their most fulfilling path.

Holographic seeing comes from being the "universe in a drop". It started to happen after a series of wakened dreams.

After decades of being well practiced, it's become second nature. I've also found that it is an innate ability that almost everyone I've worked with has on subjects for which they have

4 Nassim Haramein, "The Connected Universe," TEDx Talks, June 24, 2016, YouTube video, https://youtu.be/xJsl_klqVh0.

an intimate relationship and even genius. A good example is that parents often know the future potentials for their children specifically relating to choices they are making. They also often feel what is going on with their children, when they are not even near them. Other people have the same ability when it comes to their businesses, but they don't have language for it. It's like seeing what is in the field through your cells.

I just have a lot of practice with it. Even so, there is a wonderful study that illustrates the point with people that don't even have a lot of experience seeing this way. Stanford University published a study on remote viewing.[5] The study took average people, taught them the skills of remote viewing, and watched as non-gifted people remotely viewed realities that were not in front of them with 80 percent accuracy. How could they know? What's the scientific explanation? In my experience, the answer is holograms.

Our Innate Abilities are abilities that are prevalent when we are living in flow. Another word for Innate Abilities is superpower. The mastery of these abilities is essential to *staying* unstuck. They are what allow us to thrive. Think of them like skills essential to living in your groove and part of the advanced operating systems that run the most powerful computer in the world—you.

Shifting an entire paradigm on any subject is an Innate Ability called a Brain Bridge. In a holographic fractal Universe, you can shift one person's paradigm, which allows all of their beliefs to up-level at once. It's the fast track. This is why I get so excited about Brain Bridges.

---

5 Russell Targ, "Remote Viewing at Stanford University in the 70s," *Journal of Scientific Exploration* 10, number 1 (1996): 77–88.

The Brain Bridge That Changed My Life

After working with Brain Bridges for a short while, I experienced a huge paradigm Brain Bridge that changed my life so much I couldn't even work on belief-shifting anymore because my right brain convinced my left brain of such a deep, long-awaited truth.

When I say deep truth, I mean a deep truth for now, not forever. My experience is that truths evolve based on what we know about science, consciousness, and physics, so we can't even hold on to those.

As a Holographic Seer, I often see and speak paradigm shifts and find out their scientific explanation later. This was one of those cases.

I was watching a documentary called *Superhuman* (it's amazing, and you should watch it—the link is on our Resources page at https://thewideawakening.com/unstuckresources). It explains the Innate Abilities that cause us to be alchemical. For three years, the wakened dreams I was having showed me multidimensional DNA that allows us to access non-3D abilities, and junk DNA seemed to be connected to the mystery in my dreams. Junk DNA does not encode proteins like regular DNA, therefore for a long time, scientists didn't know its function. I started to understand that it did have a function which I will talk about more below. I was so inspired that I created a program about our superpowers called Innate Abilities, as I mentioned previously. Science is currently showing that multi-dimensional DNA is quite possible and even likely, but that is for another time and book.

More importantly for me is an interesting experiment that the FBI demonstrated in the *Superhuman* documentary.

Ben Hansen used to work for the FBI and now runs around the world looking into detecting instrumental transcommunication (ITC). Most people think that sound waves are how communication happens and a tape recorder will pick up on those waves. Makes sense. But most people don't realize that our words, thoughts, and voice also transmit electromagnetic energy. So, when you speak, you can pick up on electromagnetic energy and play the electromagnetic message through a player that offers the exact same message as the sound waves did on the recorder. Since your electromagnetic voice can be picked up by an induction coil, that means humans can pick up on your words without ears to hear. You are affecting others, and they are affecting you as you are an inducer and electromagnetic being. The point of this is that the Earth, the solar system, and your body are all electromagnetic in nature and inductive. You are constantly communicating your frequency, mood, and level of awareness and it is being imprinted on the world around you; the world around you is influencing you as well. Yet another way we are, again, connected. This is how we can think of someone halfway around the world, and they can call you.

Shifting the paradigm about how deeply we are connected to Life and each other, and that it is explainable scientifically, left every belief I had in question. I started to hold my beliefs very loosely. I became much less interested in what to believe and far more interested in co-creating with other creator friends. I mean, how much fun is that!?

Like Rob in the earlier story, I completely changed my relationship to what I was teaching. I was just 3D and doing my best to have the most optimal beliefs that I could. Then

I realized that I had the same spinning toroidal field that is the source of my life at the core of every proton in my body. I saw that from the smallest part of my existence to the Universe at large, everything is intertwined. I realized that we could shift a lot faster than we had experienced prior. This is when life and my courses started to get interesting. I didn't want to work on my beliefs anymore. I wanted to change whole paradigms because then all of my beliefs and thoughts would shift.

If I could find deeper truths that set my rational brain free, I would find freedom at a whole other level. If I could find a way to remind my whole body to function at the level of remembering that I contain the Universe in a drop, then life would get delicious and expansive.

Hence why this book is such a passion. Brain Bridges are a paradigm shift for how we evolve. We use other tools that put you on the fast track to thriving beyond Brain Bridges. I will teach these in our programs and books to come.

Each chapter can be thought of as an independent Brain Bridge on a new, significant subject from here forward.

Allow yourself to experience the stories and descriptions in your cells.

Keep your grip loose on the safety mechanisms and control traits that keep you in never-ending loops. Allow yourself to consider the paradigm shifts in the twelve chapters to come.

I can't wait to hear what happens. To explore your options and become a member of the Heaven on Earth Construction Crew I invite you to visit https://thewideawakening.com/.

CHAPTER 2

HOW TO BECOME A MASTER AT RECEIVING

*"We have the capacity to receive messages
from the stars and the songs
of the night winds."*
Ruth St. Denis

Who birthed you first? Your parents? Or Life itself? Did your biological, earthly parents dream up the idea of you, or did Creation conceive you before you came into this world?

The answer to this question matters. If Creation dreamed you into being, then your original parent is not physical. This means you **received** your body, your cells, and a house for your spirit as your first act of mastery.

How powerful! Your spirit accepted this body as your first act of receiving. Receiving is your nature.

It's no wonder that we are so adamant that our earthly parents should have known better!

Your first experience with parenting was with an unconditionally loving cheerleader of your awesomeness who never got distracted from helping you thrive, no matter how nasty or ornery you got. Creation is the ultimate example of the most Divine parent. If we can distinguish the Divine parent as different, first and foremost, from earthly parents, I think it might help reduce pain and stimulate compassion.

Remember the story of Rob, in chapter 1, who found out that placing Creation-level expectations on fallible humans only causes upset? Similarly, the idea that our earthly parents should be unconditional cheerleaders with perfect hearts, knowing exactly what to say or do in any situation, is not productive and just isn't logical. Consider that they had absolutely no experience in doing that themselves or in witnessing *their* earthly parents doing it. When you make the shift in perspective, you can start to relinquish the blame and shame toward your parents and toward yourself as a parent. You can also start to receive what your parents offered you through a different frame of reference.

Italian automaker Enzo Ferrari had a dream of elegant high-performance cars, and the engineers made it a reality. Creation had a dream of you; the conduits through which it came were your earthly parents. Just like Ferrari was always championing his cars to evolve and be their best, Creation was always by your side. Because this is a holographic Universe, this dream is within you at all times. When it feels like you can't access it easily, it is because your survival-based operating system has put you in the mode of, "I am alone," and Life always responds, "As you wish."

The perspective of feeling like you are alone in the world, or misunderstood, won't feel the greatest (or contractive, as I've mentioned before). This feeling is your greatest guide: your body, telling you that you are out of sync with your highest and best path forward. Even feeling contractive is receiving from your body's connection to greater wisdom, letting you know that the perspective that you are alone is suboptimal.

You are a born receiver, and you are always receiving. You can't help it. However, your translation of the information you are receiving may be a little off or a lot off, which will result in struggle.

You Are a Living Intention

There are several paradigm shifts up for renewal in this chapter; one of them is to let go of the idea that you need to intend to be fulfilled. Instead, recognize and accept that your very life embodies the intention you seek and is worthy of fulfillment.

After receiving your body, this vessel for your spirit, the next major act of receiving is receiving the most unconditionally loving, wise, no strings attached, nonjudgmental, completely neutral supporter of your greatest life that you could ever have.

Your greatest source of optimal guidance is whatever you call that omnipotent, omniscient force of Infinite Wisdom that continuously creates. Again, at birth, you were a genius at receiving what you needed, but I wonder, at what age do you think we stop experiencing life as miraculous and creative? Our brains, when we are developing as children, operate at different brainwave frequencies to assist us to learn and grow. Between the ages of zero and two years old, our brains are in super receptive mode (without critical thinking), or Delta, and between two and eight, we are in Theta most of the time, or a state of super learning and imagination. On average, at about seven and a half years old is when you start embodying critical thinking, and so the imagination starts to fade.[6]

6 Amanda Gachot, "Understanding the Brainwaves of Your Children," Up All Hours, 2020, https://upallhours.com/article/understanding-the-brainwaves-of-your-children.

Current understanding in neuropsychology suggests that as children, we exist in a more open state of brain activity as our prefrontal cortex is developing. But it's not until the age of eight that we start using that prefrontal cortex to filter the information we are receiving. Otherwise, you would still be wide-eyed, in love with life, playing with possibility, and looking at it all like an adventure.

But here's the secret most people don't know: you can get that sense of wonder back, regardless of your age.

You are an essence with infinite life pouring through you in this physical reality. As such, you are on a trajectory of potential outcomes that match your genius. You are a living intention from Creation and were such long before you came to this life. Life knew exactly who you were and could become. Creation is constantly creating upon what it has created before. Life thought you were a good idea now, based on what is currently happening in the world, the cosmos, your area of genius, your personality, and the future potential for expanding more goodness in times of great change.

It is quite significant that your Essence is pouring through that body, born into that family, that culture, from that history of past lives, and given our current reality. You are not fated for specific outcomes within your path (e.g., being a dentist or a snake whisperer). You are being called, however, by a slew of possibilities that would be optimal venues and opportunities through which your skill sets and personality traits would cause the greatest feeling of fulfillment for you, while offering your glorious contribution to this world, and beyond.

At this point, you may be asking the questions, "Is there such a thing as fate? Do I have free will, or not?" As it turns out, the answer is both yes and number

In other words, you are always guided toward your path of most fulfillment and best use of your areas of genius. Your life matters, and it is critical you are present to these voices of the heart in these times.

In being the creative force that you are here to be in 3D, there is an ever-present feedback loop, with you as a fractal of Creation, feeding back to the whole. You are in a dance. You send information to Life, and it responds in kind with unconditionally loving feedback. When you receive it, your path forward feels expansive and possible, and when you don't receive it or misinterpret it, your path feels contractive and hard.

What if you're just a Cosmic Three-Year-Old here to play with the resources on Earth, and use all of your abilities, and expand upon the beauty that already is? Then the entire way you did what you did now exists for all time in "the field," and can be accessed metaphysically by all. Likewise, you are able to receive wisdom from everyone else's experience.

Your personality traits and protective mechanisms may have done their jobs by isolating you or protecting you from potential danger in the past, but they may have also kept you from receiving. When you apply yourself fully to the life in front of you and let it rip, that same doorway (no longer guarded by old, unneeded protective mechanisms) that lets your true essence out also lets Life's wisdom in. Or, when the protective mechanisms are present, they keep Life and flow from entering.

Isn't it interesting to consider for a moment that if that's true, then your life is now being pinched off, or bottlenecked, by a paradigm of protection that's inconsistent with who the Universe knew you to be before you got here?

It's an ingenious mechanism to notice when you feel contraction or expansion. That simple practice can let us know if we are on track, in alignment, and moving toward contribution, meaning, and fulfillment.

Deserving What You Receive

This will be short and sweet.

The Universe is not set up based on your needing to deserve what you receive.

You didn't have to do anything to receive the air you are breathing right now, the trees that give off the oxygen and transform carbon dioxide into oxygen. It all happens without a thought or concern for your lovability, acceptability, or awesome personality.

It is an entirely humanmade construct that we get water or air or are loved by Life by working for it.

However, we live in a benevolent Universe!

This is not to say that doing what feels good in your heart, appreciating more, being present to your blessings, and making contributions that give you joy are not pathways into enjoying what you receive. But enjoying what you receive is a completely different idea than the act of receiving itself.

You may hold a belief that has you thinking you must deserve something before enjoying it. My question to you is: does that thought feel contractive or expansive? If it feels contractive, then that is a surefire sign that it is more than likely an incorrect assumption that will take you off track and lead to a less fulfilling life.

Receivers in Your Body: Telomeres

The next concept will help you understand how much is given to you and how you are already *set up* to receive.

On the end of your chromosomes, tiny structures called telomeres assist in intracellular communication. They help electrochemical and biochemical messages go back and forth between your body's cells. When this communication is fluid and unrestricted, you will feel alive and youthful. Certain lifestyle choices and toxicity in the body can directly affect the length of your telomeres; they can get shorter and, over time, less responsive, but that is changeable. Once the telomeres shorten to a certain length, they signal that cell into cell death, which will ultimately result in your body's death.

Telomeres are held within the nucleus of your cells and receive chemical messages that actually instruct your glands and organs how to behave based on the messages from other cells and given the biochemicals that reflect your personality's interpretation of the world. That's how much your perception matters. Your body is a direct translation and operates in the image of what you allow yourself to be inspired by, loved by, or afraid of.

Another way of saying this is that *how* you receive, or the filters through which you receive, matters as much as *what* you receive.

Some studies have shown that taking certain nutrients and supplements can help your telomeres remain long and active. But the really good news is that your telomeres can also be lengthened thanks to practices influenced by the science of epigenetics, which is entirely under your control and costs nothing.[7] It turns out that, just like a muscle, you can exercise your telomeres if you want to take good care of them, and in doing so, they will become more youthful in their ability to help your cells communicate more efficiently.

What type of exercise do telomeres benefit and flourish from? What activity might change our gene expression so that we live long, happy lives?

Consider for a moment the act of using your imagination, as in "to image." The first part of imagining anything is to conjure up an image in your mind. How did you know how to "see" that image? It must exist somewhere because you pulled it from somewhere, right? Images of things that haven't yet happened are actually formed in "the field" before they take form in physical reality. The act of imagination is an act of receiving. Your brain is just a physical mass. It doesn't contain the memories; it contains the access point from consciousness for the memories. More imagination plus more creativity-based action equals longer telomeres.

When are our telomeres longest? When we are young. Understandably, science made the connection to telomere length as a predictor of when you will die. In reality, though, we have cause and effect mixed up. The degree to which you creatively and abundantly lean into the life that calls you has a direct effect on telomere length. The younger you are, the more you use your creativity and imagination, the longer the length of your telomeres. When you lean into life with zest and zeal and listen when life calls you to deal with trauma so you can move through it gracefully and get right back to creating, your

---

7 "What Is Epigenetics?" Centers for Disease Control and Prevention, last modified August 3, 2020, https://www.cdc.gov/genomics/disease/epigenetics.htm.

telomere length does not shorten as quickly. I call it living like a Cosmic Three-Year-Old (or C3YO in my world).

My logic also says that telomeres are just like my flabby triceps. If we don't use them by being fully creative and acting on our inspiration to create, then we are not going to the gym for our telomeres. Think of how often you have tried to control life so that it would stand still. Your body responds to that perspective as though you are ready to retire, so there is no reason for my telomeres to be long, as we are not using them. From that perspective, there is no need to be creative, therefore no need to be connected.

I am living proof of that at fifty-six years young. I work out more than I ever did when I was younger, and my body knows that I am interested in energy flowing through it and ideas coming to reality because I am constantly engaged in creative projects using my imagination. (I'm just not working on my triceps enough, clearly.) The more you imagine and create, the more you are behaving like you want life force pouring through you because there is much to live for. When you ask your body to come alive, you ask your telomeres to engage, for your cells to speak to each other. The intracellular communication is being activated, much like when you work out your muscles get circulation and develop, to fulfill your dream or dreams. This is why the traditional idea of retirement, as many define it, is overrated. As long as you are doing things that have meaning to you, your body must respond.

Remember, you have 37 trillion individual living entities called cells, and each and every one of them said yes to housing your spirit. Your cells are alive and talking to each other because you chose this life. Give them a job, and your telomeres will be well activated.

You are built to receive.

Receivers in Your Body: Photons

There are fascinating German and Russian studies on photons and how we send and receive them from and to each other. Photons are tiny information packages communicating about you and others that are picked up by receptor sites on the outside of your cells.

Photons travel around the world seven times in a second. That's quite a bit faster than sound waves through speaking. Imagine how much more important evolution thought this kind of communication was compared to sound waves. This cellular communication via photon packages of light is, to me, part of the scientific explanation for intuition and instinct. Other scientists are discovering that what was once referred to as junk DNA may also play a role in this communication. There is more to be learned, but it seems clear to me that your entire body was designed to be a sender and receiver of photoelectric and biochemical signals.

What if we could hear that communication? What if we are already going direct in connecting to Consciousness, but we're so busy in our head trying to micromanage the degree to which we get hurt or judged that we're missing the simplicity of it all?

What would that feel like?

Imagine that Life thought that it was so important for you to be connected to the quantum field of Infinite Wisdom that it gave you 37 trillion cells that have receptor sites on the outside of them to receive photons and a way for those same cells to emit photons.

Consider this: we only have one mouth and two ears.

Does that give you a sense of how important receiving from Life might be?

Never mind the fact that you have 2 telomeres per chromosome, 46 chromosomes per cell, which makes 92 telomeres per cell, times 37 trillion cells in the human body. We truly are receiving machines, but we run around trying hard to deserve it when it's not a deserving-based Universe.

When I started to understand the power of that paradigm shift, my first thought was that perhaps this is a scientific explanation for intuition. Since then, I realized that there are many additional possible scientific and mathematical explanations for intuition.

If you want to be unstuck, wouldn't it be essential to learn the language of Life? The Quantum Field in which we are situated is filled with information that transcends what the brain can access, but your cells send and receive photons from your greater mind, which is directly connected to that information.

This is what happened the first time one of my clients went from frustration to receiving mode in a second.

A Story about Starting to Receive

I was teaching an intermediate program called The Thriving Operating System. Although I say it incessantly, sometimes I take for granted that everyone in that program knows that:

1. I am not their guru.
2. You are remembering yourself, not fixing yourself.

One of our students, Judith, kept asking the same question in different ways: "But how do I stop beating myself up? How do I stop judging myself? What are the steps to change my negativity?"

Judith lived in a part of Asia at the time and was surrounded by a lot of drama. I realized that the issue to be addressed had nothing to do with her questions. It had to do with the Survival-based Operating System of the one asking the questions.

So, I said to her: "Judith, listen, did a perfectly expansive Universe birth you? Did it consider all time and space, every speck of dust, and every atom that ever was and will be before your essence came into that body?"

She said, "Yes."

I asked, "Did that omnipotent, omniscient creative force give you free will?"

She said, "Yes."

"Are you the thinker of your thoughts and the asker of your questions?"

Again, "Yes."

"Are we trying to always be happy in this program, or are we embodying our ability to thrive through whatever happens? Are we attempting to have predictably great outcomes all the time in our lives, or are we in this life to experience miraculous outcomes? In other words, do you want to survive or thrive?"

She said, "Thrive."

Then I asked, "Then what would someone who is thriving ask, instead of questions about fixing herself, given that you are a freewill thinker of thoughts? And who would have those answers, you or me?"

She said, "Oh, I see what you're saying. Well, they would ask: How could I feel better right now? How can I have grace for well-practiced habits because I haven't quite embodied new ones yet? And I can get those answers because you aren't my guru."

Judith switched from asking questions about her brokenness to how she could thrive.

The answers she started receiving were now about her thriving rather than surviving. She then expected answers related to her shifting gears in her life.

And yes, it takes practice. Just like telomeres and triceps, you have to go to the gym. And yes, of course, she needed help with asking better questions because the trauma she had experienced caused her to have well-practiced neural networks that constantly looked for people, places, and things that would hurt her. However, we are either the thinker of our thoughts or the victim of them.

Totally different energy that nets you with totally different results.

She would not have gotten the results she was looking for from our program if we hadn't had that discussion.

It's the same reason that people go to some practitioners for decades or spend so much money on "fix me" endeavors because they are focused on problems while spending such a small amount of time, if any, on how to actually thrive.

By making that slight shift, Judith soon got new clients, and her interest in self-criticism stopped within a couple of weeks.

She shifted paradigms just from one five-minute conversation.

She is one of our greatest fans.

Consider This

The instant that society, your parents, the TV, school, your place of worship, or your culture showed you that fitting in, being a certain kind of mom, having your kids be happy, not failing people are more important than following your greater wisdom is the instant you started surviving. It's also the instant you stopped letting love win and stopped receiving solutions that would let love win.

This includes love for yourself, like in Judith's case above.

Remember that the life you are given is for you to receive.

Finally, there is no need to superimpose your knowledge on someone else; it simply takes their power away to receive from their true source of wisdom within.

Breathe.

The Ingredients for Receiving

Take spaciousness or receptivity breaks. If you are too busy, you will not be present enough to do what life is presenting you; you won't even see it. Receptivity breaks happen when you go and do something fun or uplifting for absolutely no reason. You are telling consciousness that you are interested in receiving those 'or betters' because your frequency is high, and you have relinquished control, so the door is open. Raising your frequency of emotion is like changing the channel on your TV. What you receive is entirely dependent on the channel to which you tune your emotions. Receptivity breaks are an opportunity to change your frequency channel.

To receive, you must have an understanding that you are being given to at the rate of trillions of cells at a time and that it is all happening for you.

You also need vigilance for the direction and good stuff that life is sending you, rather than vigilance for protecting or proving yourself; if you are too independent, you will miss all of the opportunities for cocreation and contribution. These opportunities that present themselves are often nonlinear and a little irrational to the left brain. But when you leave consistent, intermittent space in your schedule, you can create receptivity breaks.

The last step is to be willing to dance with whatever life brings you by saying yes. That requires being curious about the adventure, which you actually have been on before. You did all of this when you were two years old.

Consider that the illogical can often get you to more fulfilling and more efficient levels of flow, given that the quantum field has access to all of the resources in Creation, and your left brain only has access to your history.

Action Steps

Collect evidence to tell consciousness that you want to master receiving. In your *UNSTUCK and Thriving Playbook*, write down three ways that you were given to, without asking, in the past twenty-four hours. (Get the *UNSTUCK* and Thriving Playbook here: https://thewideawakening.com/unstuckresources.)

WATCH: The second step of receiving is witnessing the amount of time in the day you spend trying to control, feel safe, and carry the world yourself. You cannot act from self-preservation or independence disease *and* receive from Infinite Wisdom at the same time. Doing it all yourself is also an act of telling consciousness that you prefer to be alone.

For the next twenty-four hours, watch. Don't observe, witness, narrate, participate, or try to interpret what's going on around you. Simply watch, with no attachment, to anything or anyone. Even "noticing" is more effort than is necessary. At first, this state of nonattachment may be challenging to achieve for any length of time because we're not used to allowing what we see to exist without trying to make some meaning out of it.

We human beings are naturally and understandably judgment machines or fixing machines. We are so well-practiced that we have created crystallized neurosynaptic highways in our brain that become hardwired for being independent. But as a sovereign being with dominion over your body and mind, you get to choose whether to go down those neurosynaptic highways or not.

By the way, you're not allowed to use this exercise to judge whether or not you're doing it correctly; this is not about collecting evidence about how broken you are.

You are not broken, and you don't need fixing. Remember?

However, from time to time, simply watching may assist you in understanding or experiencing a different perspective. Stay curious like a Cosmic Three-Year-Old.

Receive what you receive from this exercise. Then grab our *UNSTUCK* and Thriving Playbook so you can keep track of your experience.

CHAPTER 3

THE FREEDOM OF VIBRANT HEALTH BEYOND YOUR GENETICS

"Genes are not destiny."
Dr. Bruce Lipton

Have you ever wondered why some people don't get the same diseases as others in their family?

Have you ever asked yourself why more women than men get MS or thyroid disease? Why do more men die of heart attacks than women? Why do more women than men get breast cancer? If we are so biologically or cellularly similar, why do men get ALS more than women do?

Why is diabetes more prevalent in the African American population than other groups of people? Why have gluten, sugar, and dairy intolerances become such issues for increasingly more North Americans?

The answer lies in understanding that your genes are expressed based on the biochemistry that triggers them. Just because you have a gene doesn't mean you will get the disease. So, what is at the core of why some do and some don't?

I thought, probably like you, that your genetics will dictate what happens to you later in life. I also thought you could manage how long it took before you got arthritis, the severity of hot flashes, or the seriousness of prostate cancer through nutrition and being positive.

Now I know better. I didn't realize then that I had control over ninety percent of what went on in my body. According to Dr. Bruce Lipton, less than 1% of all diseases are truly genetic. His book *The Biology of Beliefs*, is life changing. It's about epigenetics, amongst other profound ideas. Epigenetics truly changed my paradigm of health. You can shift your biochemistry and therefore which genes are expressed can shift to a great extent.

Most people think of genetics as what drives the car of our physical development. In fact, our individual genetic makeup is merely the road map; *we* are driving the car.

Dr. Bruce Lipton, a geneticist, says: "When we understand that genes are just respondents to the environment from the perceptions handled by the cell membrane, then we can realize that if life isn't going well, what we have to do is not change our genes but change our perceptions. That is much easier to do than physically altering the body. In fact, this is the power of the new biology: we can control our lives by controlling our perceptions."

Our genetics give us a whole galaxy of possibilities of physical expression from which to choose. It's our biochemistry that triggers the genes that give us our health. The genes don't do it on their own. And there is something governing our biochemistry.

What governs our biochemistry? Over 90 percent of your biochemical expression is governed by how you receive external inputs, like upset, stress, love, change, food, trauma, sunsets, and so on according to many epigenetic experts, like Bruce Lipton. The perspective with which you receive those things changes the chemistry in your body and therefore changes which genes are expressed. Over time, it can also change the genes themselves.

Epigenetics is the study of how our behaviors and environment can cause changes that affect the way our genes work in our bodies, not gene sequencing. 'Epi' meaning above. Once you understand the mechanism of epigenetics, you'll have the key that unlocks the door to your personal freedom. You'll be able to free yourself from the thoughts and beliefs that no longer serve you, some of which weren't even yours to begin with.

Often these self-limiting beliefs have been handed down to you by your culture, family, ancestry, or even your religion. You never consciously chose them. They were, in a sense, bequeathed to you to take on as your own personal reality or as a subconscious act of loyalty to a parental or authority figure.

But it is entirely possible to step into a non-karmic, non-ancestral plane of existence by owning and putting into practice what science tells us about how powerful you are when it comes to your health.

Isn't it time to throw off those shackles and regain your sovereignty and dominion over your most precious asset, your body?

We Are as We Think

Our biochemistry results from how we think about the events that happen or have happened in our lives and how our social network subtly trains us to plug into certain realities based on preconceived notions of morality, ethics, or personal integrity. This is one of the reasons that some of us have difficulty finally ridding ourselves of past trauma. We are generally surrounded by people who agree with our perspective on life.

This is why, in families, the same genes seem to express, hence the same diseases express.

The effects of distress affect our emotional well-being, and more significantly, the imprint of that ordeal on the brain causes it to cook up a neurochemical response that we can call a protective mechanism. That protective mechanism is what your brain will default to whenever a similar event happens; therefore, the same chemicals are produced over and over.

For instance, whether school was a good experience or a challenging one, the perspective you held about school will generate certain biochemistry until you die, unless you shift it. For example, I went to High school and was tall, awkward, incredibly shy and had acne. I also wore square glasses and my curly hair was not my friend. If I held onto my disdain and pain from school, everytime I entered a school, or spoke about school, old wounds would be triggered. I would feel anxiety. Fortunately, I have seen how beneficial my outsider status was in school. It caused me to become an independent thinker. I spent High school debating religion, spirituality and physics with my fellow outsiders. I wouldn't have so much compassion for others, nor would I be writing this book, if I hand't had that experience in school. I am so grateful for that journey, even though at the time it seemed highly suboptimal to say the least. If I didn't find peace with my experience, instead I would be living much of my life in anxiety and therefore so full of cortisol that I most certainly would not be able to "see" as I do.

That neurochemical response becomes an addiction to the body.

Nature or nurture, indeed. To break the neurochemical chain of events, you can practice new beliefs over and over again, training your body that you are interested in a different future for your health, and eventually, health will follow. You can also transcend the paradigms that gave you the health issue in the first place.

Our body loves us so much it will never lie. It is our greatest guide. When we get disease symptoms, it's like being told the painful truth by our most faithful friend. It might be painful to hear such a truth coming from such a trusted companion, but in hearing it, we can more deeply appreciate the friend and take enthusiastic action to deal with the problem.

For some of us, our first response to any ill health in our bodies might be to simply ignore the symptoms, convincing ourselves that there's nothing to worry about, that the symptoms, not given any energy, will simply pass.

But doing this, as Abraham-Hicks (a channel) might explain it, is "like putting a happy face on an empty gas tank or a flashing engine light."

The first thing to understand in this Brain Bridge is that your cells, and your health, are communicating to you about paradigms and beliefs that are living through you that have nothing to do with your most fulfilling path forward.

Your cells are trying to redirect you to the alignment of purpose, beliefs, and actions.

A simple example of this is when you start feeling responsible for the happiness of your boss, you start carrying them. Since your spirit, and therefore your connection to your innate wisdom, is flowing through your specific body, that means that you couldn't possibly know what is in the highest good for another person. You can only project based on the information you are receiving through your cells. Here, I define carrying as worrying about something or someone such that it takes up mental and emotional space in your day. So, when you are carrying, you are incongruent with your path of greatest fulfillment. The entire Universe, of which you are a fractal, never carries anyone or anything. Therefore, you will be out of sync with your natural flow if you try to fix someone else. You will have physical signs of being out of sync, like your neck or shoulders being tight, as a little reminder that you are carrying someone's life and that it's not your job.

Trudy and Health Freedom

Trudy used to work in Africa for the United Nations, leading humanitarian projects in the Ivory Coast.

People working on projects with Trudy would remark about how she always seemed to find a way to make things work when nobody else could see a path. She seemed to always be in her zone of receiving everything she needed, and it felt fulfilling and meaningful.

Despite being in a developing country and being exposed to so many social challenges and heartbreaking situations, Trudy consistently had hope for no apparent reason. She knew there was always a way, and she didn't even understand why.

While Trudy's work life demonstrated her ability to receive beautifully, her personal life revealed other challenges. She divorced a man who had anxiety problems. In her love relationship, she took responsibility for the marriage not working out and tried to change herself to be who he wanted, perceptively.

There were many chances for Trudy to be killed in the war-torn area of the Ivory Coast where she was working. She was faced with witnessing the death and destruction wreaked by conflict. Trudy was a single mother with two little girls, so she needed to get herself and her children to the safety of another country. Yep, it was that scary.

Trudy got her children out of the country without a scratch, except for the emotional scars of seeing what they saw, under almost impossible circumstances. Again, she found a way.

For her, it was an intense situation, yet a good affirmation of her ability to always get the guidance and direction she needed. For her children, however, this event likely had another effect. They understandably got trained by the trauma to be vigilant for somebody potentially hurting them or something scary happening out of the blue.

This story is not about her children. It's about Trudy's response to her role as a mother and why she started to step out of her zone of receiving and flow.

Trudy carried her children's feelings and fears about life; she worried about them and tried to prevent them from hurting while growing up in countries around the world. Even as adults, she continued carrying them. This took a toll on her spirit, thyroid, adrenals, and energy. She had to take medication for her thyroid and many supplements to compensate.

As adults, Trudy's children still blamed her for anything wrong because she taught them that she was responsible for their feelings.

Survival was the name of the game in her family. After all, even though Trudy was a receiving genius on the subject of working as a leader in third-world countries, she struggled with knowing what to do when it came to her adult kids because she was no longer cocreating or mutually honoring.

Through our work together, I showed Trudy that when we carry another, we are actually telling that individual that they don't have their own Innate Wisdom, so they stop trusting themselves. We project our answers onto perfectly good receivers, so they continue to struggle. Trudy got it.

We did some work on her ability to experience her Innate Wisdom more consistently, shifted her relationship with motherhood to guidance instead of responsibility, and worked through the truth about what happened with her marriage, a subject she still felt guilty about.

She could feel how expansive it was to give her children back their power so that they looked elsewhere for it rather than to her. She was out of Life's way.

She was also able to get off most of her supplements, and with doctor's feedback, she also got off all her thyroid support. Trudy recently told me that she has more energy than she's had for decades and is back to her clear-headed, happy self.

She watched as she went from being stressed every day to driving up north a couple of times for a break, getting out of the house more, and setting up new parameters with her daughters to have a better relationship.

In a year, during our Flight School program, Trudy had written an entire book, started another, changed her relationship with her daughter who was living with her and going through a tough time, and most importantly, began fully embracing her inner three-year-old.

She expanded her work beyond running projects and started consulting with humanitarians. She is enjoying life. She is filled with possibilities, more so than before her divorce. She sees it everywhere.

Her telomeres are tickled to be alive. I have every confidence that this will be the best time of her life.

Syncing Up with Greater Wisdom

Trudy's story was a success, to be sure. But let's dig into it: why had Trudy's body responded to the idea that she was responsible for the failure, unhappiness, and happiness of everyone around her?

Nobody could take away Trudy's can-do nature when she was younger. However, marriage and children had her tapping into paradigms about family that weren't even hers. They were, and are, society's: thou shalt carry thy children and thy spouse.

Trudy knew all along that what she was doing to help her kids didn't feel expansive, but she didn't know another way or deeper truth. As soon as she got it, within weeks, her body changed.

This is an excellent example of a Brain Bridge: frequency coherence between the brain's hemispheres, from the right to the left, across the corpus callosum.

When you are ready to shift paradigms or move across a Brain Bridge, what you feel is relief. Why? Because our entire body comes into a state of greater alignment with Universal truths about being human. Brain Bridges help us make deeper sense of difficult parts of our lives by evolving our protective perspectives about events that were scary or stressful. They change our beliefs, and (it bears repeating) this is done by shifting the overarching paradigm for greater results.

The feeling of being in sync with greater wisdom is one I always imagine to be like Jake connecting with the flying banshee in the movie *Avatar*. As a rite of passage, he must bond his hair braid with the banshee to join consciousnesses and become one with the creature. Paradigm shifts are like that. The instant you come to a deeper truth, you can fly biochemically, magnetically, and otherwise.

Imagine that you're fifty now; you're getting older, or so your history tells you. Like women of a certain age, you start getting a paunch. Or do you? I had a friend who was eighty-five who decided to change the paradigm about muscle and the elderly. Most of us think that if you are over eighty, you simply lose muscle mass and get weak and that it's just part of the aging process. She and I decided to work out the exact same amount. I was thirty-five at the time, and by the end of two months, her eighty-five-year-old strength was only 7 percent less than mine. And she was ripped! I have watched numerous YouTube videos about those over eighty continuing to physically thrive solely because they didn't conform to societal norms.

In other words, your loss of strength, ability, agility, and flexibility has very little to do with age; it has to do with perspective and what paradigm regarding aging you choose to embrace. If you stop using your body, you manifest exactly what you thought would happen as you age. Interesting, isn't it?

Right now, you may be saying to yourself, "Oh my God, now I have to notice and look out for all the thought paradigms that support my fears, and then fix them all." That seems like a lot of work, right?

That's not what we teach. Yes, you can do that, but it sounds like a lot of effort to me. Remember I told you initially that this is all about changing the paradigm of how we feel? I'm all about the 80/20 rule, which states that 80 percent of outcomes come from 20 percent of inputs. This concept was first introduced in

1906 by Italian economist Vilfredo Pareto, who is best known for the concepts of Pareto efficiency. I love to do the 20 percent of things that get me 80 percent of the results. This is about shifting the entire way you view life.

You can excavate your past until the cows come home, try to get you to your cosmic age, analyze every belief system that you're tapped into, and so on. But you know, if you excavate every paradigm you're tapped into and every pain that happened when you were little, you'll spend the rest of your life doing that because then you have *other* lifetimes to analyze as well, while you are at it.

Your genetics are not a jail, and you have the power to shift what plays out in your body at any time.

At The Wide Awakening, we do a program called The Thriving Operating System. We offer this program because going through the experience of the shift together is the best way to embody it.

I wanted to open your mind to the absolute truth that changing your biological age is possible in this chapter. I am living proof, and so is Trudy.

Ingredients for Activating Your Health beyond the Jail of Genetics

To get out of genetic jail, first, you have to know that your genes are mostly simply a road map. You are driving the car; you get to say where you go.

The second ingredient of starting to shift is that you have to be willing to do the work to change the mind that created the biochemistry. Our programs support that practice.

The third ingredient is that you must claim yourself as the expert on yourself first so that you can visit your practitioner in partnership, rather than feeling inadequate compared to their perceived authority and expertise.

Action Steps

Write down all of your roles, personality traits, and so-called responsibilities (great mom, good sister, artist, creative, adventurer, intermediary, organizer, fun person, etc.). For each of them, do the following:

1. Cross off each role you adopted from someone in your family, friends, culture, or school.
2. Cross off each role you adopted because you didn't like what a family member or friend did so you did the opposite or became different to prevent that from happening again.
3. Cross off each characteristic, role, or trait you have that was developed in compensation for a scary, stressful, or hurtful event that happened.
4. Highlight the ones that didn't get crossed off and notice what they have in common.

CHAPTER 4

FINANCIAL EXPANSIVENESS: WHAT IT TAKES TO TRULY THRIVE

*"It is impossible to be wealthy
without being of service."*
Dame Doria Cordova, CEO, Money & You™

The truth is that your natural state is one of abundance. I'm sure that a few of you might respond to that statement by saying, "If it's true that my natural state is abundance, how come it's not reflected in my checkbook?" I would counter that you are already abundant. Unfortunately, if this area of your life is an issue, the part of you that doesn't want to acknowledge how abundant you really are is trying to train your brain to collect evidence to the contrary.

Why would it do that? Well, it's dangerous to have money. People like me don't have money. Tall poppies get their heads chopped off. It's more virtuous not to have money. It doesn't matter if we figure it out because we are probably only figuring it out from the perspective that we are broken. Somehow, we operate under the flawed premise that knowing why we are broken might fix us. Right? See how it works?

The Brain Bridge around money offers you an opportunity to look at the concept of being righteous about your wrongness and carrying that with you as a paradigm you believe about yourself, your family, your life, your culture, or heaven forbid, all of the above. I knew that filter very well myself.

The second concept that we get to look at is your frequency—the level of juiciness your emotions are tuned in to—and Independence Disease.

Money is a big, fraught topic for most people because they think it's what makes the world go round. Uh, by the way, it's not. Magnetics makes the world go round, both figuratively and literally. So, if that's the case and we have beliefs about money (we all do), should we spend the rest of our lives fixing our beliefs because they're wrong? I will depart from the answer I would typically give on this subject. Why? Because the ideas about money in this world have such a stronghold on our reality that it takes a pure outlook on the subject, with no strings attached, for someone to let the past belief go and let abundance flow.

The first thing to address in the case of money is the idea that you would even spend time trying to fix what is not broken. Listen, you absolutely could be justified in some of your beliefs about money—or love, for that matter. You have evidence. Some pretty disconnected people are doing some pretty naughty and incongruent things with money.

But that's not money's fault. Remember, I started my university studies in accounting and then moved over to economics, so I understand what money is and does, and it's simply a unit of exchange. Period. It doesn't make you a better person, or more worthy, or smarter. It doesn't give you more joy or greater fulfillment. I've worked with billionaires, and they have the same problems as everyone else; *their* problems just come with more zeroes.

Money, much like clay, is to be played with. Like clay, you can learn how to create with it. Like clay, you can make cool things with it.

It's when we make money about ourselves that it gets messy. That's when we start feeling we are right about something we feel is wrong with others, or with ourselves, or with banks, or with the economy, and so on.

Many years ago, every December, during the holidays, my bank account would go down to almost nothing. I would get disturbed. Then I'd collect evidence for why that happened, as though somehow that would make it better. I discovered that you could either collect evidence for why something is happening—and therefore recreate that event in the future—or you can imagine, plan, and cocreate anew to stay in step with Creation itself, which lives in total abundance.

To be true to the quote that kicked off this chapter, my response to this time of year became, "How can I be of service?" Then, with a heart full of love and compassion, I would work at a food bank or a food line, and, miraculously, money would come in ways that I could never have imagined. It's all about emotional frequency, my friend, without attachment to the outcome.

Have you ever said one of these statements?

"I'm not good with money."

"I want to make sure I keep all my money safe."

"People do bad things with money."

"I have to guard money and control it."

"Money comes, and it goes."

"I have enough money, but never more than enough."

If any of those statements sound like you, exchange the word "money" for "some kids" or "love." It doesn't feel too good, does it? So, the subject of money will be a loaded one for most people, and therefore addressing the subject is not the first approach we want to take.

Being righteous about your wrongness (your limitations) will perpetually keep you in the same money experience. So, let's approach it a whole different way. Let's look at abundance in general. I've already mentioned that you are abundant. Here are some irrefutable facts:

- You do not have to earn true abundance. Trees breathe out what you breathe in, and you did nothing to deserve that except being alive.
- Your eyes are set up in such a way to interpret light and be delighted by sunsets of every different shade and brilliance. Again, you did not have to do anything to be worth the beauty of a sunset.
- Your cells renew anywhere from once every three hours to once every seven years. Again, there's nothing you have to do to make that happen. You have an abundance of new cells without even knowing about it.

So, abundance is not your issue. Where you focus is the issue.

Everything that comes into your life enters because of your magnetics (what you focus on) and your frequency (the "goodness" of emotion you experience). In the case of money, if you know you have a lot of history and baggage on the subject, the best place to start is to find a different subject on which you can easily experience joy, creativity, and energy. Then, aside from making sure you have a plan to pay your bills, don't focus on money, especially if you have perspectives that bring you down or make you worry about money. Instead, focus on other areas of life that lift you up, do things that inspire you, and fill your day with acknowledgments of your abundance (which may or may not be related to money) in ways that are easy for you. Raise your vibration.

Wherever you last left your frequency on any subject will affect your ability to receive in that area. If you haven't changed your relationship to that subject, it's best to enjoy another aspect of your life in the meantime. Enjoying your life in one context absolutely opens doorways in others as long as you don't bring your attention to subjects that you haven't transcended yet (like money).

Here's a story that is a great example.

Debt-Free by Dating?

Let me back up a little. When I was in my early thirties, I was in debt to the tune of about $32,000. I lived on my sailboat. I didn't own it, my bank did, and I even had the loan document to prove it. It was an asset of a sort. I was struggling. I didn't know anything about physics or magnetics or how the Law of Attraction worked, so I did what most of us do in that kind of situation: I created a list. On it, I logged all the money I owed and to whom, and I placed that piece of paper on the door to the "head," the boat's toilet, where I could see it every day as I got ready to go to work. I looked at that list every morning, hoping it would inspire me to do something different to alleviate my looming financial crisis. It didn't. All it did was make me feel more depressed.

Around the same time, I decided to act on a completely different problem. Up until then, all my relationships had failed. I had convinced myself that I had been picking all the wrong men. My epiphany came when I considered that it wasn't my partners who were the problem; after all, the only common denominator in all of them had been me. Maybe, just maybe, I was the reason these relationships hadn't worked out.

I decided to embark on a journey of discovery about my relationships with men. I also had to admit that part of my recipe for relationship failure was that I had been trying to fix the poor bastards I was dating so I could feel safe, instead of being curious and on the adventure of discovering love.

To test my theory, I created a game. My plan was to date someone new, platonically, every night for thirty days. I would go on the dates, stay curious, and have some fun; I would hold it all loosely. What a concept! I did just that and had a ton of fun. I went rollerblading (it was the '90s), and I went to movies, and out sailing. One man and I even dressed up as opera characters and went to *La Bohème*. It was so fun! I played. It helped me deepen my appreciation of the dude gender so much, given I knew so little about men. I had grown up in a family surrounded by my sisters and my mom. Even our dog, Muffin, was a girl. My dad was out doing the provider thing quite a bit, and I kind of put him on a pedestal. He shared little about himself back then, as he did his best to keep his masculinity intact in the sea of estrogen that was our home at the time. And I have to say, as dads go, he spent lots of time together with us water-skiing, playing T-ball, skiing, and doing other fun family stuff, so he was there with us. I didn't get that he had a different operating system until right before I went to university. He said,

"Jennifer, be careful of guys at this age, they don't think like you." Too true.

After experiencing dates with some cool men in different social situations with no agenda or pressure, I concluded "Hey, I really like men." I played with the concept of simply being present, enjoying my dating partners as they were, instead of fixing them. I realized that just because they weren't like women that didn't make them inherently scary or wrong.

One lovely man, who had a boat on the same pier as me, started to catch on that I was getting dolled up every night. He would sit at the end of his boat, waiting for me to walk along the dock to my car. He always had a smile on his face, trying to communicate his amusement or curiosity. One night, as I walked past his mooring, he summoned the courage to speak to me and asked me what I did for a living.

(I don't know why I didn't think of it before, but as I write this, it strikes me that he might have thought I was a high-priced escort. Hahaha.)

I told him that I was a sales manager, which was true then. I thought he might be curious about the fact that I went out every night, so I explained to him my theory and the game I had created to test it. I could tell he was interested in me, as well as my little story, but as a thirty-one-year-old hottie, I had little interest in this "old man" of forty-four.

He told me that he wanted to participate in my experiment, but I had already picked the men I'd have dinner with. He was, in a word, relentless, and every night I went out, there he would be on his boat, wishing me good luck and imploring me to go out with him instead of those other guys. Finally, I gave in and let him take me out on a date. He arranged for something that had been on my secret dream list for as long as I could remember: a ride in a hot-air balloon. It was an awesome evening.

At the end of the date, he leaned in to kiss me, but staying true to the rules of the game, I turned my head. I made sure that each man I went out with understood and agreed that these were to be purely platonic dates with no physical intimacy. I could sense that he wanted something more than just a casual night out. He had told me as much during dinner; he was ready for a committed relationship. I told him I was not. I was still committed to playing my game of self-discovery. When I went to bed that night, I admitted to myself that I was, at the very least, intrigued by this man.

We started to have regular conversations, deepening our connection. He understood that one of my strengths was as a business consultant. He hired me to consult for his company and paid me $15,000. That contract was enough to erase half of my lingering debt. Incredible!

And no, it was not that he was trying to buy me. He didn't know I was in debt. I wondered then: were love, fun, enjoyment, and money related? Or was my abundance showing up because I felt so incredibly expansive about men and dating?

I know now that both statements are true and intertwined.

I might have sucked at finances at that time, but I kicked butt at playing a game of self-discovery with no attachments. I had been fully committed to my little experiment, which enabled my magnetic field to recalibrate and become a match for the abundance I had been seeking. Flying high, loving my life, having fun, and holding it all loosely became the frequency of everything I had ever asked for, including my eventual marriage to the man with a boat.

I didn't try to fix my money consciousness; money hadn't even been the focus of my little "game." I had only been committed to the journey of discovery, not as a strategy to access more abundance, but to become an active and willing dance partner with the Universe of possibilities. As a result of that dance, I was able to gain more financial independence.

Sometimes, working on a specific problem will yield little net result. We sometimes laughingly refer to it as "pushing a wet noodle up a hill." No matter how much you try to move the noodle, it still squirms under your fingers. Shifting your focus towards a subject where you have little to no emotional resistance will often provide a more positive outcome from a nonlinear perspective. Pick something that's easy to play with or something you're curious about, and go on the adventure of discovery.

Once you are in the flow of the entire Universe, you naturally line up with the operating system of thriving, and you'll start to notice miracles becoming normals that are often completely unrelated.

If you don't like the color of the marker you're writing with, don't get angry at the marker because it's not the right color. Pick up a pencil instead; shift your focus.

This is the time to break free from any idea or concept that says money has anything to do with your value, worth, or lovability. I understand how difficult it can be to shift your focus and change your internal belief system around money. Even the word "money" comes with lots of mental and emotional baggage. But I've consistently found that almost everyone I know who's wealthy thinks of money as a game or a tool. They put no more importance or value on their money than that. It's just something they play with.

At this point, it's important to point out that this book is made up of words on a page. In and of themselves, they are little more than individual characters inked or scanned into a sequence intended to make sense to your rational mind. They hold no power by themselves, so if you're reading this book hoping to glean some type of hidden knowledge so that your life feels better to you *without you doing any of the work*, you'll be sorely disappointed.

The magic comes from the work.

You can't integrate what you don't feel, and you can't change what you don't willingly integrate, no matter how ugly or uncomfortable that might be. The most transformative and powerful thing we can do is understand and own where we are without recrimination or guilt. If you've read this far with the intention of understanding, then you'll know that to transcend your current reality, whether it's to do with money, health, or relationships, you must first get real with where you are emotionally. Then you must deploy an intention and emotion greater than—or of a higher frequency than—your current reality.

You can get intellectual information anywhere. You can read rational ideas and step-by-steps and strategic plans about finances but still get no further in your pursuit of abundance; indeed, many options are available from respected authorities.

You came to this book because something about it spoke to you in a language that only your heart understands. That's about magnetics.

In the debt days of my previous story, my list on the head door and doing the same things I'd always done before only deepened my depression. It stalled any forward momentum that my actions might have created. I took the list of debts down. It was getting me nowhere fast because it reminded me every day of my struggles.

I let it all go at that moment—all the concern and worry I'd been carrying in my heart. I didn't know what else to do, so I decided to release all my expectations and attachments to any outcome and shifted my focus to something I could feel playful about—my curiosity about men and the dynamics of dating. I didn't realize at the moment of that decision that I was saying to the Universe, "All right, show me."

"Show me" are the two words that I first said out loud when I left my husband, the man I met in the story above. These two words didn't occur to me until I was open to hearing the answer. The right people, the right resources, the right circumstances show up as soon as you authentically speak these words and feel that you are ready to live your "most fulfilling life, with the greatest amount of contribution, with the most efficiency, and meaning while enjoying the abundance of all things you desire."

Most people who have been misunderstood in their lives try to figure out life on their terms, becoming fiercely independent. When someone becomes independent, they start to believe that they can, or should, figure everything out by themselves. They close themselves off from receiving support from anyone else because nothing is ever given freely based on their history. It often comes at a cost that's too high.

This belief snare isn't about abundance per se. However, it *is* about receiving. I realize that we covered the basics of receiving in the previous chapter, but it bears repeating that when you're willing to let go of "your way" you become a blank slate for the Divine.

Once I invited the Universe to "show me," I decided that I would work on my love life instead. I decided to change my relationship to men. I couldn't change my relationship to money because I didn't know what I was doing. I could be playful about my dating game, but the money issue seemed so heavy at the time that I couldn't figure out a way to make it less dense, emotionally speaking. Once I started enjoying the game and the men I was meeting, I had a great deal of fun and expanded the joy in my life. It took my focus off what wasn't working. I was letting the entire Universe in. Not only did shifting my vibration in this way work, but it's also the way things are supposed to work.

When times get the roughest and toughest, that's when you must be courageous enough to ask yourself, "Am I willing to do what it takes to get into the miracle zone or flow again?"

Here Are the Ingredients Necessary for Financial Flow

Let's make a distinction between the little you—your ego or personality—and the larger you that is consistently connected to Consciousness and All That Is. The little you thinks it wants something because it thinks it will be happier or more complete with it—or, more accurately, that your life is incomplete *without it*. That belief will instantaneously take you out of your natural state of abundance because wanting that thing makes your life focused on what it lacks. Wouldn't it serve you more to embrace the perspective of the larger you and consider that you have a body that loves you? Isn't it more powerful and freeing to focus on the friends or family members who *do* love you?

You are a function of the entire Universe. The entire Universe is expanding out without any resistance at all. It assumes abundance, it assumes all the raw materials are present, it assumes the resources are available, it just keeps creating upon itself. You are a focal point of that very Universe. The fundamental truth about abundance is that it's already within *you*; it's not a destination you're journeying toward.

To find your flow with financial abundance, you need to do some groundwork first.

- Make sure you're vigilant—and I mean wired—for the abundance that already surrounds you. Until you automatically experience life that way, experiencing financial overflow will be difficult. How you view and experience the world will override any intentions you may have around effortless financial overflow. If your underlying way of experiencing life shifts, everything else has to go along with it.
- Don't put yourself in a position where poor financial flow will be in your face all the time. That's the same thing as when you have gained ten pounds, and every ten minutes, someone comes by to tell you that you're fat. Not cool. Not helpful. And certainly that won't net you the result you want, metaphysically speaking. Get into a situation that gives you breathing room.
- Enjoyment is key. Allow it to be experienced.
- Have a plan, as it will keep your monkey-mind at bay, as long as you follow it. Over time, find people who can help you with better plans.

In addition, there's one ingredient we haven't talked about yet: generosity. Generosity is knitted into the fabric of the

Universe. The Universe is overflowing with ideas and possibilities and creativity. It does not withhold. Generosity in the form that I'm speaking of is unconditional. Its reward is the glee you'll feel simply from giving. Another equally valuable unconditional act of generosity is receiving with grace instead of false humility. Remember, every act of generosity is only an act of generosity if you feel that it's mutually honoring. If you feel that it costs you while you're benefiting another, it isn't an act of generosity. It might, instead, be an act of conditionality.

Whose definitions of abundance are you comparing yourself to? Which seems more expansive, Life's expansive version of abundance or society's version?

Would you be willing to let go of the idea that you need to fix your relationship to abundance? Most people have a relationship to their lack instead of their abundance. And you can't fix what you don't have.

Are you willing to engage the idea that you already *are* abundant and then practice feeling that way so you can live in a completely different vibration?

As you begin to understand and embody how abundant the larger you truly is, you'll start to notice all the little ways the little you previously sabotaged those joyful feelings of celebration and let them go.

Here is one last story to make the point from a colleague who used to do workshops training people about leaving room for miracles in their lives. One of his workshop participants complained about how he never won the sales contest at the end of the year. He was tired of always seeing someone else win a Mercedes-Benz, and he was complaining about how he had always *wanted* a Mercedes-Benz.

The wise sales trainer turned to him and said, "I want you to stop focusing on how you don't have a car, how it's always frustrating, and how someone else always wins. We're going to do an exercise for next year. What kind of car do you drive now?"

The workshop participant owned a crummy, beat-up green Vega hatchback. It was rusty and didn't even have wheel covers anymore.

The trainer said, "This is what I want you to do until I see you next year. For the next year, I want you to treat your car the way you'd treat a Mercedes-Benz."

The guy replied, "What am I supposed to do? Wax over the faded paint and rust? Put expensive synthetic oil in it too?"

The trainer said, "Yes, that's exactly what you're going to do."

"You want me to put premium gas in it?"

"Yes," the trainer told him.

The guy ended up having a lot of fun with his car. The people at his local gas station would laugh their butts off as he put premium gas in his bucket of bolts. Over time, they started playing the game with him and having a blast. He started to get into the idea of treating his car just like a Mercedes-Benz. He went so far as to buy some nice floor mats for it, and one of the floor mats covered up a rusted-out hole in the floor quite nicely. Funny, right?

But guess who won the Mercedes-Benz at the end of the next sales year? He did.

He didn't win the new car because he manifested it. He didn't win it because he was focusing on a Mercedes-Benz. In his mind, he was enjoying himself so much that it stopped mattering. And, by the way, after he won, he kept his old car.

At first, he had just been doing his assigned homework. But then he started to have fun with it all, and the result of putting himself into a vibrational match of enjoyment and expansiveness about his car was abundance. For him, there was nowhere to get to and no attachment to any outcome except enjoying and appreciating what he already had.

What if the enjoyment *was* the abundance? What if enjoyment equals abundance? What if it really is that simple?

Action Steps

Put in some time on this exercise to expand enjoyment.

Write the question "How can I enjoy this moment more right now?" on twenty sticky notes and post them all around your house, your car, even on your bathroom mirror. I want you to be thinking of answers to that question all day long, and especially before you go to sleep.

Play with it! Put on music while you do housework, or gargle your water as you rinse the toothpaste out of your mouth, making it a game. You might slow down eating your meals so that you notice textures and flavors more.

When paying bills, write a little note to the person receiving the money expressing your gratitude for the service they provide. Even if you can't make the full payment, write, "It might look like money, but this check is a unit of my gratitude."

There's nothing to get right, and you cannot get it wrong.

CHAPTER 5

FINDING HARMONY AND FLUIDITY WITH FAMILY

*"Most of your family will not be related to
you. If you're lucky, they will be.
Either way, does it really matter?"*
J. Hough

The beginning of this Brain Bridge happened in a previous chapter when I spoke about Rob, whose mother catalyzed him to create Soul family through his friends for the rest of his life.

"Life knows exactly who your family will be, and most of them won't be related to you." It bears repeating. If you look at your life, you probably had an instinct that this was true. Look at how you relate to some of your friends, how much you share with them.

Maybe it's time to stop wishing your family members were something they're not. Heck, in more cases than I can count, our clients end up being born as guides for their parents, not the other way around.

Remember, you already have at least one unconditionally loving, behind you all the way, always in a good mood, cheer-leading and guiding, omnipotent parent from which life came, and It/She/He is not related biologically to you either.

Once you can start considering that your parents are not responsible for your happiness or unhappiness and are either catalysts or guides, a lot of freedom can happen in your relationship with them.

No, this does not absolve them of responsibility if they were abusive because that's definitely not okay in any Universe. This chapter is not a way for you to skip good old-fashioned therapy either if you need it. However, do consider that from Life's perspective, if you didn't get what your heart desired one way, it's waiting for you in another form.

If you're a parent, apply the above considerations to your relationship with your children.

I don't know about you, but for me, it seems that almost all problems in any relationship, especially the ones with biological family members, can be traced back to the expectation that since they are bigger than you, they should know better.

Nope. Assuming that your parents haven't done in-depth self-awareness or personal development programs, you can expect them to be the way they were, except even more practiced at it. If you don't do anything to change yourself, then you'll be practicing unproductive habits for longer.

In survival-based communication, your words will sound protective or defensive.

Emotional triggers left over from previous relationships and concerns for safety, protection, equity, or sovereignty all tend to contain hidden conversational landmines, ready to blow the whole thing up before any real consensus can be won. These unresolved issues can make dealing with those you love very tricky and can bring up every reactive and unproductive pattern you've ever had.

However, the real question is this: how do we ensure our default way of being is completely lined up with how the

Universe saw us before we got here? Are we congruent with and living our life in that vision? Are we completely free from the judgments and issues in previous relationships, familial or not?

Before you have an important conversation, ask yourself, "How old am I right now?" If the answer is anything less than your current age, it's not time to have the conversation, or it will attract scenarios from the past playing out again. Have you ever noticed that?

What if you showed up in every relationship free of your history, clear and in your heart? How would you act if you were emotionally removed from how other people may have treated you in the past, separate from what anyone may have projected upon you? Can you let go of what happened to you when you were sixteen and any meaning you made up about it? Who would you be at that moment?

How would you communicate with your kids, parents, uncles, or cousins if you didn't have to look for threats to your sovereignty constantly?

When you experience yourself as the Universe sees you, your commitment to manipulating people to like you or behave differently toward you disappears.

One day, when I was four, I decided to "help" my father in the basement. He was shaping a piece of wood paneling to put around the fireplace. My dad likes to be meticulous in his projects, probably because his father had been an engineer. My dad took the jigsaw and cut the paneling to fit perfectly into its allotted space; he did it with the spirit of "measure twice, cut once."

He laid the paneling down to do a couple of other things. While he was busy with other tasks, I took the hammer and whacked off a corner of the paneling. To my shock, he was not happy. He yelled at me. My four-year-old mind was thinking, "This is not going well." It all felt very scary.

Then I thought to myself, "Maybe I need to do something. Perhaps I need to change my behavior because he's bigger than me. He must know better than me, but he's behaving in this loud way. I thought he loved me up until now, and now I'm not sure. I thought I knew what love looks like; people are nice to you and they're proud of you. And he's not."

And then I thought, "I guess I've got to change—I guess I've got to figure out what makes him happy, and then I'll be lovable again."

I spent the rest of my life trying to manage my actions so I'd be likable. I didn't want to make anyone upset. Which, for someone like me who is born to be a tree shaker, that's like trying to stuff a pineapple into a flower vase. It's hard!

I'm sure you've had a similar experience sometime in your life. Most of us have had many of those; we're either not enough or way too much for some people to handle. Some of us can't even fully connect with those kinds of incidents because they hurt too much. We get really upset sometimes with our parents, especially as adults, and sometimes we get upset with our kids.

I'd like to share an awareness that changed my life, my relationship with my parents, friends, stepdaughter, and sweetie.

Have you ever noticed how we create expectations of our children or parents? If you don't have kids, this won't apply, but I'm pretty sure everyone can relate because we've all had parents or significant caregivers.

Just for a moment, connect with and fully feel an expectation you might hold. If it's difficult to imagine those emotions with your parents, for whatever reason, maybe you'd find it fruitful to connect to a judgment you hold about someone else, perhaps a neighbor or coworker.

I've heard this a lot from clients: "I wish my parents had been more supportive. They should have been more fun-loving. If only they had seen me, I would have had so much more confidence. If only I'd been unconditionally loved, I would have doubted myself less. If only I hadn't been criticized, then the outcome would have been different." Blah, blah, blah. You get the energetic resonance of those kinds of thoughts, right?

"Oh dearest," Life said, "your biological parents did not birth you at all. You might be the product of your mother's womb or the communion of a sperm and an egg, but that's just the three-dimensional mechanics, the engineering of it all. The truth is, you're not a function of those mechanics. The truth is this: who you really are started as a sparkle in the eye of Infinite Wisdom. You—the essence of you, the idea of you, what you look like in this physical package, even who your biological parents were going to be—are a result of Infinite Wisdom. It realized that the world is going through a huge awakening, a massive moment of great change.

"To be successful in that awakening, Infinite Wisdom knew that to facilitate this change, it would need participants, cooperative components, who would be willing to see things in a new and different way. You are here now because of the courage required for remembering who you really are and where you truly came from. We need you and others to relentlessly return to their hearts. Considering any spirit and soul that could have come to the planet at this time, the Universe thought, 'Hmmm, I think you're perfect for the job. As the winner of this cosmic lottery, you get to be a piece of that puzzle of expanding Heaven on Earth.' Then, and only then, did your parents bring you into this world.

"What would love do, Jennifer?"

What *would* love do?

Sandy and Her Family

Sandy, one of my clients, has also become a dear friend. She's one of the most heartfelt and courageous people I know.

Her family is her remaining siblings, as their parents died years ago.

She ran a healing center in Canada and was having issues with her sister because when their parents' estate was decided, her sister did not abide by the guidelines that their parents had laid out. There was a house, and her sister thought that it belonged to her because she had been living there. But really, all three siblings needed to split the proceeds. The discussions were heated before doing our work, and nothing ever got resolved.

As Sandy and I started talking about her sister and the situation, I said that her family might not be related to her. With that insight, she realized that her sister was definitely of another soul family. Yet from that place of understanding, she could feel more compassion for her sister. They simply had two different operating systems.

I looked at the hologram of her sister, and it was clear how much fear she had and how much she loved Sandy. Sandy and I looked at a specific point when her sister was devastated about the loss of her parents, and we saw that it wasn't about greed—it was about losing the last bit of connection to their parents.

That's where their conversation started this time, and they both agreed to learn the tools we teach about letting love win. Eight years of strife were resolved in less than thirty minutes. It took relinquishing their expectations that biological family members should have similar beliefs, finding compassion, and letting love win.

Sandy and her family are getting ready for the holidays as I am writing this paragraph and have created a celebration of their parents' lives. In honor of coming together, they're making the same family meal that their mom used to make.

Now that's an 'or better.'

Ingredients for Finding Fluidity in Family

One of my favorite movies is *How to Train Your Dragon*. In the movie, the kid's name is Hiccup. His father, Stoick the Vast, puts an older man, Gobber the blacksmith, in charge of Hiccup. After a particularly embarrassing mishap by Hiccup, Gobber waves his hand in the boy's general direction, chases after him for a while, and says, "You know, Hiccup, if you're going to have to stop all of ....this." To which Hiccup replies, "But you just pointed to all of me!"

"Yes, that's it," says Gobber, "You need to stop being all of you."

Maybe you felt like Hiccup at some point in your life, and you've been defending yourself from criticism or harm ever since. Maybe you've come to believe that someone else's opinion of you is the truth of who you are.

Maybe, like me, you morphed yourself so that you'd be lovable or acceptable to others. Maybe, just like Sandy, you react when you don't feel connected and aren't looking for the "third entity" solution to the problem.

Maybe you're not well practiced at answering the question "What would love do?"

In the movie, the audience finds out that Hiccup becomes the hero only when he fully accepts who he is and uses his unique abilities to free his people and the dragons. It's an entertaining parable, and it happens to be true. Hiccup discovers just how hard it is to live up to someone else's expectations if that means living against his true nature.

Soul Family doesn't need you to change. And some of them can be biological family if you're fortunate.

The Universe sees you as completely perfect, no matter what you're going through. It doesn't have a problem with anything you say or do, and when you're a little off track, it redirects you without judgment to something that might serve you in your highest a bit better.

Would you do the same for your family? "Don't judge a fish for its ability to climb a tree." I love this quote! There are lots of fish in your family. Fish are okay too.

Save yourself some misery, and don't project the characteristics of a perfect Universe onto mere mortal parents. They're either your guides or your catalysts, the ones you're guiding or simply those you appreciate for giving you life, and that's all. Sometimes they're a little of all of it.

What then would you have to relinquish to do what love does?

Action Steps

Your job for the next twenty-four hours is to pick three people in your family and write a note of gratitude to each one of them for being exactly as they should be. Before you write the note, take a moment to get grounded, then open your heart wide and express yourself from a place of love. You might want to express an apology, regret, appreciation, or unconditional love. Then release all expectations or attachments to get a response or acknowledgment.

On that note, give your love freely.

Now you know what love would do.

CHAPTER 6

LAW OF ATTRACTION 2.0

"Your life will be as good as
you allow it to be."
Abraham-Hicks

Manifesting probably doesn't mean what you think it means.

Each and every second of every day, you are manifesting. Everything you receive is a manifestation. You didn't mentally intend 99 percent of what you live; it's in your beingness. When you do the work to change how you operate in life, you change what you believe, think, and manifest.

This chapter is all about understanding that what we call miracles were always meant to be "everyday normals."

To manifest doesn't mean intending something into being. It doesn't mean attracting a certain outcome. Certain characteristics of the Law of Attraction (LOA) are important to understand, as they give context to why you often don't get what you envision. The characteristics are:

- The trajectory for your life, when you were born, is a divine intention in and of itself. You were born in the spirit of making the most fulfilling use of your skills and living a life of meaningful creation, and that divine intention will always override your mind's intention.
- The Infinite Wisdom has way more resources than you do in 3D survival mode. Survival mode has us in heightened anxiety and producing more cortisol, therefore, our

ability to be intuitive decreases proportionately. Meaning our ability to receive what Infinite Wisdom has to offer as solutions, decreases proportionally. What you manifest will always be far more wonderful than what you intend. In fact, you are designed to transcend your vision board's version of reality.

- Your entire life, every day, is a manifestation. You didn't deliberately ask for any of it, but you did allow all of it through your path of the highest frequency. If you want to know where your frequency is on any subject, look at the things you've manifested. Your frequency is where you want to spend your time.

From a multidimensional perspective, manifestation is a simple process, but to the human brain, it seems so much more complicated. Creating a manifestation requires far less work than most human beings realize. There's almost no work involved at all because if you're living in the manifestation zone, things come to you naturally. The first step to entering that zone is to get out of the way of the natural processes of the Universe.

Creation is happening without your mental intention. Since you *are* a spiraling intention, that way of operating naturally leads to precession or new ideas when you meet others.

Here's a wonderful story from one of our Get Out of Your Own Way™ classes that illustrates this best.

Did I Manifest a Truck?

Jackie was a cool chick. Her family owned a construction company, so trucks were really important to their ability to thrive. She loved to create things with her company.

After a great day of conversation on day one of Get Out of Your Own Way™, Jackie got super revved up about the idea of manifestation. She explained that even though she loved her work, had a great family, and was, for the most part, pleased with her life, she had always struggled to manifest what she needed.

When she returned the next day, she said, "OMG, Jennifer, you won't believe this. My son was cleaning up my office, and he found a three-year-old vision board. The biggest picture on my vision board was a red Ford F-150 pickup truck. And my son looked outside and pointed out that the truck I'd put on my board was the exact truck I had in the driveway three years later. I totally manifested it!"

Did Jackie manifest that? Sure, sort of. I did have to clarify the idea for her though. I'm such a party pooper.

This is what I said: "Listen, Jackie. It *is* kind of cool. Seeing holographically, I want to offer you what I see when we manifest things, so to speak. Are you open for an upgrade in your paradigm about manifesting?"

Jackie replied yes.

"Okay," I said, "Here goes. The trajectory you're on as a soul, based on the skills you have and the choices you're making within the realm of free will, is sending you in a certain direction. The passion with which you do everything is also juicing up your journey and keeping you at a certain frequency. Your greater consciousness already saw that the natural outcome of that journey would eventually result in that truck. So, your greater wisdom made sure that the picture of what was already inevitably going to be your truck found your hands and your scissors on the day you did your vision board. Why? Because it knew we would be having this discussion in Get Out of Your Own Way™ so that we could clarify how much the Universe truly does have your back and how much easier the Law of Attraction is than how it's been described. Everything you know you want and, more importantly, stuff you don't even know you want is already coming into form in nonphysical terms as a potential based on everything you're living. Your job is to get out of the way and do the work (and the play) to live at the frequency where what is waiting for you can come. That's how easy it is."

It was such a good day.

Jackie loved this new perspective on manifesting and has since become even more proficient because she stopped working so hard at it. The Universe has your back—and you contain the microcosm of its alchemy within you.

All That Is held the dream of you until the time was right for your arrival, a time when enough people were asking for you and the medicine you brought with you. Once humanity was ready, the multidimensional doorway was opened, and you came into being.

In other words: you yourself are a manifestation.

What Ingredients Are Necessary for You to Become a Manifestational Genius?

Here's the thing: this chapter is not about how to create a manifestation portal. It's about how to get out of the way of your own manifestation portal by judging less and learning the practices that will have you embody your natural state of receiving all that is inevitably coming your way.

What affects your natural state of receiving?

Earth revolves around the sun at about 67,000 miles per hour as the solar system flies through space. Earth is a three-dimensional sphere and is made up of concentric spheres of nickel and iron at its core, then liquid rock in the mantle. That sphere is covered with the crust, made of tectonic plates that move against one another on the planet's surface. Finally, there are the layers of water on the surface, and above the planet is the atmosphere, which is formed of gasses and is retained in place by the spinning of the Earth's innermost core. The spinning creates the gravitational field that keeps it in place, all while the atmosphere protects life on this planet by shielding us from the intensity of the sun.

Our planet's gravitational field is also affected by the moon, which creates tides in our oceans and bodies of water.

Earth is spinning on its axis around the sun in the Milky Way galaxy, which itself is spinning in space at the outer edges of a Universe that is expanding out through a process that involves dark energy, which scientists are only just beginning to understand.

This entire dance is occurring at the exact moment you are reading these words, and in the next moment, and in the next, without you needing to do *anything*.

Similarly, your body is made up of 37 trillion cells, each with its own energy source, vibration, frequency, and magnetic field, all working in concert on your behalf without you needing to do anything, save being a good steward of your resources.

At the core of each cell is the active double helix strand of DNA that contains a blueprint or road map filled with "codes" about your body that may or may not be expressed. There's also DNA that was once thought to be dormant or inactive that scientists have called junk DNA or "non-coding DNA." They originally called it junk not because they were able to figure out that this material is left over from some other type of division, but precisely because they hadn't fully figured out why this DNA would be in our bodies in the first place. Without a reference point to explain its function, scientists in the past deemed junk DNA as less important than the 20 percent of DNA that was explainable, hence "junk."

Scientists have since discovered that this junk DNA does some amazing things in your body. Much of it has to do with cell replication, sequencing, and RNA. And this is all happening without your mind needing to intend or control. Imagine if you had to intend all of that! You wouldn't have time to eat!

Do you wish that your life was different? Do you compare yourself to others, or the vision you have for it? How often are you distracted by what-ifs instead of dancing with what-is? All the while, the Universe is looking to serve you with what's in the highest for you, consistently. Your not-so-junky DNA has your back, and it's doing its thing and assisting in replicating your cells so you can keep on creating.

You don't have to ask for or earn what your body does for you all day, every day. That's exactly how the Universe works. "As you wish" is what the Universe says to your every heart's desire unless you want to work harder to prove your worth. That's up to you.

Oprah and Me

I had tried for years with my friend Lois to get tickets to see *The Oprah Winfrey Show*. Our efforts didn't result in tickets, just frustration and lots of phone calls.

My clients often said to me, "That's because you should be on *Oprah*." Kind, but it didn't help me get tickets.

So, I just forgot about the idea. After all, my life wasn't going to change from seeing Oprah; I'd just be going on a fun trip to Chicago. Or so I thought.

Within a few months of giving up on the idea, I found out that a friend was featured in Oprah's magazine and had written an article; a colleague was an advisor to one of the shows; and my editor, Susan, was also going to be on the show.

At first, I was annoyed, until I realized that Life was trying to tell me something. By getting out of the way and not trying so hard, I was getting closer to my tickets.

Within a week, a totally different friend who didn't even know how long I'd been trying to get tickets phoned me and said she had tickets and did I want to go? Um, yes, please. Yvette and I had so much fun in Chicago, but the story is so much juicier than that.

I got there, and they were premiering a cartoon movie (which I love), and the stars were Carol Burnett (my hero), Steve Carell (my future hero), and Jim Carrey (definitely my fave), all of whom were interviewed on that episode.

I got to watch the movie in Oprah's theater with the audience privately.

I got to meet the stars.

I had already been introduced to the producers of *Oprah* two weeks earlier through a friend who had no idea that I would be there two weeks later. He connected with me, and we had a meeting in Chicago right after the show. It was fabulous.

After that, of course, everyone had already left Oprah's gift store, so I had it to myself and the staff. I went to Oprah's closet, which consisted of clothing and items Oprah had worn that she was selling as a fundraiser for her foundation. To my delight, Oprah's closet contained size 12 clothes (I was a size 12) and size 9.5 shoes (also my size).

To my delight, Oprah's staff helped me get dressed in a whole bunch of Oprah's clothes. They then asked me what I did for a living. I told them, and they asked me to give them a mini-workshop.

So, there I was, doing a private workshop for Oprah's staff in her store, wearing her clothes and some rockin' boots. (I still have them. I've posted a picture of them on the Resources page. They are gorgeous. Just saying.)

Talk about an "or better!"

Needless to say, yes, everything can come to you. I had only wanted to sit in Oprah's audience; I hadn't asked for any of the other incredible things that happened.

This is what's possible for you too, and I'd love to show you how.

Action Steps

Just one action step for this chapter. Easy-peasy. Ready? List five times in your life where 'or betters' manifested without you needing to ask. You can start with number one, which is every function in your body that happens without the need for your intention.

CHAPTER 7

RELINQUISHING YOUR RESISTANCE

"You can go kicking and screaming,
or you can just go."
J. Hough

W hat if you had no resistance to fulfilling your dreams and doing what seems hard?

I remember being resistance-free when I was a kid.

I'd watch the news with some friends of the family and think to myself, "I don't understand why people fight. Don't these countries see that everyone wants to get along? Don't people know that they can just talk to each other and work it out? What I'm seeing on the TV isn't how I know the world *could* work."

My friend's father would often tell me that's not how the world works.

That's how resistance starts: with one person telling you that life is not magical or alchemical.

We resist the truth about how magical life can be because we don't want to fall too far. You don't fall far if life is just okay. It might begin as a defense mechanism against being the odd one out, but after a while, the dissonance between what you know and what you see slows your vibration down to deal with the density around you. At some point, it becomes purely about survival in a world that is often hostile to who you really are and the living possibility that you are.

Modern airplanes need some air resistance to fly, but too much resistance will cause them to crash and burn.

The Universe is constantly expanding out. So is Consciousness. Consciousness is always creating upon itself, experiencing itself through its creation, namely you. And there is no resistance big enough to stop Creation. There's contrast and resistance enough to knock a planet into another orbit, but it's all part of the flow.

Take a moment and ask yourself these questions: Am I an expression of the entire Universe, or not? Of all the possibilities that exist in the quantum field, didn't I win the cosmic lottery so that I could be here at a time of great change because there is so much opportunity to create? Doesn't that mean I'm a piece of the puzzle of Heaven on Earth?

How much longer are you going to believe the fallible, limited perspectives of human beings in your constellation trying to be comfortable in your presence? Wouldn't it be more fluid, and much less resistant, to believe that the entire Universe thought you were a good enough idea to bring you forth?

Here's a story that helped me truly understand what it is to live without resistance and the alchemy that can happen as a result.

First Class All the Way

I was flying from Albany, New York, to Texas with a lot of questions. I'd had some pretty synchronous experiences in upstate New York whereby I kept meeting strangers I had so much in common with, and I truly wanted to know the mechanism by which these things manifested.

I didn't quite get yet what "doing what life presents you" was. I mean I wasn't thinking about meeting all of those cool people—it just happened, or so I thought.

I was about to get a Grade A lesson in relinquishing resistance.

While being driven to the airport, I had an awakened dream. It was very instructive. The dream indicated that I was meant to relinquish judgment about anything that happened while I just followed the threads of the ideas that came to my head at the airport. I was to simply do what was in front of me to do. What Life was presenting me. I didn't realize that Life was going to answer my question.

The Albany airport is small and easy to navigate. I was sitting at my gate and realized that I would be in economy for a long flight. I'm five feet ten and really need space, especially when I'm going to something work-related. And I was. I looked at my ticket and realized that my seat was in the middle. I knew I had to change it.

I rushed up to the counter and asked the lovely lady whether there were any business class seats, and she said number The man who was up at the desk right before me got the last seat. I looked at him and snarled playfully, and he laughed.

I then went back to sit down and wait for my section to be called. The section at the back of the plane. Ugh.

"Thanks for the exercise in futility, Life," I thought to myself, wondering why I hadn't manifested a better seat.

As I was getting on the plane, to my left, I noticed a woman in a window seat in first class with a dog on her lap. I love dogs. I thought, "Man, that would be so cool." The seat next to her was empty so far, but I was headed to row 27.

I realized there wasn't going to be room for my carry-on, so while the flight attendant wasn't looking, I put my bag in a vacant spot in the overhead bin in first class. Well, at least there was that.

I walked back to 27B and scrunched myself in. This whole time, I caught myself resisting and just letting it go. I remained curious on the adventure as best I could.

All of a sudden, I saw the man who got the last first-class seat walking toward my row, but he wasn't looking at me; he was looking at the guy in the window seat.

He laughed when he realized that I was sitting beside his colleague, and he shared with me that he'd moved to first class, hoping that his friend could upgrade too. He looked at me and said, "Unfortunately, he and I have to go through some work documents before we land, so would you mind taking my first-class seat so I can sit beside my friend?"

Um, let me think about it. Joking!!!

I got up and went to sit in first class. His seat was the one next to the lady with the dog. When I sat down, I remembered that I had already put my bags in first class. And then the dog jumped into my lap and stayed with me the whole trip.

This all fits under the category of "You can't make this stuff up!"

Oh, and did I mention it was free? So, I didn't pay for first class either.

There's an exclamation point on this story that defies survival-based thinking.

The lady next to me told me she had the dog because she was prone to migraines due to a head injury, and she was heading to a conference about how to heal. She was one of the speakers there.

I shared with her that I used to have migraines and had healed entirely. She asked me to teach her some of the tools and techniques I knew because flying was one of her triggers. So, I did, and they worked.

At that time, I was running my clinic in Canada and spoke about biochemistry and how it's affected by our emotional filters. She asked me if I'd like to speak at the conference or a future one. I told her I'd love that. It paid $10,000, the most I'd ever made speaking at the time.

I think you might be starting to get the picture.

I was over the moon about following what Life showed me in my awakened dream.

I couldn't wait to teach my students even more about resistance.

What did I learn that stays with me to this day?

- Life has our back, if we choose to see it this way.
- Everything happens for us, not to us, and sometimes we'll have no explanation for why it happens the way it does.
- Life loves to surprise and delight us as long as we stay curious on the adventure instead of resisting what we don't prefer.
- Resistance is a human construct. We can choose to resist because it doesn't fit our pretty picture, or we can stay in the flow of what's happening.
- Resistance is useful sometimes when we aren't ready for what's coming. Sometimes we need time to breathe before we do what Life is presenting us, and sometimes we can just say, "Bring it on."

What Ingredients Do You Need to Relinquish Resistance?

Every year, we lead a program called Flight School. It's eight months long, and it includes retreats, group coaching, one-on-ones, and interviews with a whole host of amazing leaders of the Awakening. I met one of my favorite examples of living without resistance on a retreat to Maui with a Flight School group several years ago. Let's call him Pete.

Pete lived a life without resistance and leaned into his creativity with a level of yes-ness I had never experienced before.

Now, here's the thing about seeing your life as a piece of art: all you want to do is create. That's all you want to do.

I talked to Pete about his upbringing and all the twists and turns it took because his family was dirt-poor. You'd never know that by how he lives now.

I said to him: "To the rest of the world, it might look like the secret to your success is your positive thinking or plain good luck. It seems to me that early on in your life, you recognized who you really are and weren't afraid to live that truth, even though it meant leaving behind everything you knew. The other point that I'm present to, hearing your story, is that you didn't or wouldn't believe anyone who tried to tell you who you were or should be. You've been very courageous in your self-belief.

"That's not about positive thinking or putting effort into thinking positively—it's about remembering who you really are and then acting from that truth. You can't help but be positive when you remember who you are! In fact, when that's the case, how could you be anything *but* lit up, turned on, and excited about getting up in the morning?"

Pete lives his life with almost no resistance to who he really is. His life is such a great one to illustrate the point of this chapter. He doesn't entertain any 'buts', 'ifs', or 'maybes', hedging his bet on life, constantly creating his art as the piece of the puzzle of Heaven on Earth he came here to be.

I don't want you to hear this story and immediately start comparing your life to his. I'm going to remind you that you are not broken and don't need fixing. I simply wanted you to hear what's possible when you live this way.

Pete told me he has healthy resistance, which comes when trying to solve a problem with a design, in his house, or with a project. He also said that kind of resistance always catalyzes him to create once more.

If you're going to argue with the fundamental truth that you are here because you have something to contribute and create in this world, then there will be a ton of resistance to who you are pretending to be. However, if you're willing to go on the adventure of discovering who you really are and the sense of meaning that awaits you, you're going to find yourself subconsciously relinquishing a lot of resistance and subject to a lot less headwind.

If you knew, in your heart and to the tips of your toes that you were a piece of the puzzle of Heaven on Earth, you'd be relentless about acting on possibilities too!

If the Universe wanted to put together a Heaven on Earth Construction Crew, wouldn't it be composed of people who thought differently than anyone else? Wouldn't it be natural that other people would judge them negatively for not fitting in? At some point, wouldn't they start connecting with others just like them? Wouldn't they be finding the books, leaders, and the teachers who would encourage and embolden them? And since their work consisted of living on a planet with the density that constantly opposes them, wouldn't it be necessary to remind them, from time to time, that they're all pieces of the puzzle of Heaven on Earth?

Well, I'm reminding you.

Maybe you thought your job was to shake people's trees. Maybe you stopped shaking trees and withdrew because you got judged. Maybe you change yourself for others. Maybe you've done that your whole life and just realized it now. Maybe you've shaken the tree so much sometimes that afterward, you feel like you need to get away by yourself, push the reset button and reintegrate yourself.

I kind of like shaking trees when it seems called for. Leaning into Life means that you will shake trees, even if you aren't trying to. If you are in someone's life that is challenged by you being you, remember that everything operates on magnetics. They asked for you. Don't resist; just stay curious.

If you're reading this, you were likely born to follow your heart's calling, or else your heart wouldn't have called to read it.

Resistance is futile. The simple truth is that the world, your essence, those that have lived before you, and the Universe asked for you during this time of great change.

Action Steps

Simple.

Write down three specific areas of life where giving up on resistance would be a good thing for all concerned and how you will go about replacing resistance with being curious on the adventure instead.

You might need to call a few people.

See you on the adventure.

CHAPTER 8

YOU AND YOUR GUIDANCE AS ONE

*"You cannot teach a person anything;
you can only help them find it
within themselves."*
Galileo

That title, "You and your guidance as one," is a bit of a misconception. It presumes that you and your guidance are somehow separate from each other in the first place. The truth is, your guidance is present in this and every moment, even if you're not aware of it.

Back in chapter 1, I wrote that in a fractal Universe, the Wisdom of all that exists is actually hidden in plain sight in the patterns in nature and all around you. In every atom is the information of the original atoms from which they were birthed. Let's take time to visit the space between the atoms where possibility lives by meditating or going for a walk in nature. There is "a field where we can meet," where all knowledge rests that allows us to create that which has never been before. And we are made of those patterns, those atoms, and those spaces between the atoms. That wisdom is a part of us at every level.

The paradigm shift in this chapter is really about shifting our relationship to the realms that some feel are very esoteric, like guides, angels, and elementals. What if our minds construed them as separate entities because we were taught that we couldn't possibly be that superpowered? Not in an arrogant way, just in a matter-of-fact way. It's simply a misinterpretation of the nature of what it is to be human. We were born to access the genius of pure potential.

Because our superpowers pour through this body, this life, this history, this ancestry, this culture, and this time in history in this neighborhood, our superpowers are differently expressed for each unique person. We were not born to belong to or fit in with each other—we were born to discover the maximal use of those superpowers. How do I know? Because there is never more energy rushing through us or more "yes" in our life than when we are using the gift that we are to create.

It's about belonging to the Universe as a Unique Creator, not trying to fit in with civilization.

The irony? You never feel like you fit in until you realize yourself and the gift you are and unapologetically go for it.

Every time I was sick and dying (all five times), it was clear that when we fully choose to be here, as all of the deliciousness that we are, something happens. For me, when I was on a table in a hospital in Ontario dying of meningitis, I woke up once in the seven days I was in a coma. The only time I woke up was when my former husband and my boyfriend at that time, who both loved me, were holding my hands on either side of me. That was a miracle that I opened my eyes to. Love did that. Love has seriously powerful juju.

Meningitis did something to me. Honestly, my ability to "see feel hear" holographically got amplified because I had lost my memory, so all that existed was the present moment. If that hadn't happened, I would have been too scared or skeptical to let my other dimensional aspects show me that this way of see-ing the world was possible.

That's when I started understanding human superpowers over ten years ago. I started seeing the metaphysical mechanisms that cause us to intuit, change the energy of a room, be magnetic to desires, lose relationships with people, and get out of sync with ourselves. I started seeing how incredibly connected we are to others, nature, and the dreams we have. That's when people I didn't even know started to come to me without marketing or writing books.

I'm going to get a little vulnerable here. Before I got meningitis, I wasn't listening to my Innate Wisdom or using my superpowers to their greatest extent. Sometimes I'd take them for granted and go against my inner knowing. And the more I followed the path of metamorphosis from accountant/economist to teacher of applied physics and multi-dimensional DNA, the more Life showed me when I was out of synch with that direction. I would have struggle and conflict occur (either through a health, staff, or money issue showing up). I was never *not* told verbally that I was off my path, but Life made it very clear when I didn't listen.

This is how I ended up in the Bahamas with my then boyfriend, spending all night crying for no reason. I was supposed to be going home, as I had a flight booked. Logic said there was no reason I shouldn't fly home. I had never had such powerful and direct messages about not leaving (and I've had plenty of them since). Consciousness already knew that I would pick up meningitis sometime on my way home.

I flew home despite the overwhelming feeling not to leave the Bahama's. The first day home I seemed fine. The next night, as a "courtesy," my former husband came over to tell me he was moving in with his girlfriend, and the next morning I was convulsing in front of a client, and my staff was calling 911. My guidance said not to go home, but I did.

I would have gotten the same upgrades to my superpowers by staying in the Bahamas. Alas, I didn't understand at that time what my greater wisdom felt like.

But let me tell you, I do now.

From that time on, I understood our Innate Abilities in a way that is so matter-of-fact that sometimes I can't believe other people don't see it. I feel blessed because those abilities enable me to navigate the world with tremendous confidence.

Which is part of the reason I teach what I teach. We can all have that much confidence. The world is not a scary place when you can "see" what is going on, and you know you'll have everything you need to not only navigate it but change it.

Since that moment, I've sought out people who have felt their intuition rising, people who know they're awakening but don't fully understand it, people who know they're experiencing new superpowers but don't know how to use them, people who feel their hearts calling them to more but have no idea how to get there. I help them to embody what they need and get out of the way of the life that's calling them by showing them how.

I've noticed that there's a mass awakening of these abilities right now. I'm committed to the idea that these abilities are *no big deal*. They aren't. We were born to be that connected to Life. And all sorts of people are sharing with me that they're getting intuitive hits, or downloading ideas, or channeling some kind of wisdom. I do all of that stuff. But it's not a big deal. It's not special. It's who we are. Thriving can only happen if we feel connected.

YOU AND YOUR GUIDANCE AS ONE

Some people are thriving and using these abilities all the time—they just don't call them superpowers. They merrily go along their way and thrive, and I will never meet them. But I bet you know a couple of them. Everything comes to them. They're always appreciative and clear-minded. Opportunity abounds for them.

Our clients include a wide range of people, such as executives, salespeople, parents, construction workers, shamans, and political leaders who are starting to know that embodying their ability to navigate this world in a ridiculously connected and abundant way is what they are being called to. They cannot *not* go on the journey.

Someone once said that being part of the Universe is like being the finger of the hand of God. I like that analogy. Even if we all come from the one hand, you'll notice that none of the fingers look or act exactly the same. I think of it more like a symphony, all born to channel our brilliance through the instrument of our body and life.

We've had a misunderstanding that goes something like this: We've been told that God is somewhere out there. We've been told that our guides are out there. We've been told that the angels are out there. We've been told that greatness is out there. Even the ancient mythologies say that somehow there's something that comes down from the sky, and it's better or bigger than we are. Even when we worshiped the sun, we separated ourselves from it. But when we separate ourselves from our Innate Wisdom, when we separate from our angelic playfulness and ability to manifest and protect, when we separate these realms from us, when we say guidance is out there, it's different; it's not with us. When we need to spark their attention because somehow they're not always there for us, we misunderstand how the Universe works.

You have so many connections to the other dimensions that allow you to be superhuman (well, actually, normally human, if we are honest). In the Survival Operating System, there's no request for superpowers because you're just using your brain and senses to create. Three-dimensional senses for three-dimensional survival-based living. When you relinquish your need to survive and you get the slightest bit interested in the Thriving Operating System, all of a sudden, you have more energy. Now, you're more connected with all of the dimensions of yourself, so the energy moves through the universe in abundance.

It's like giving up an addiction to a predictable life.

> *"Every time you don't listen to your*
> *Inner Guidance, there is a sense of spiritual*
> *deadness. A loss of energy."*
> Shakti Gawain

Going Direct and How I Met My Husband

It was the summer solstice in Maui and my birthday. I lay in the grass with light rain falling on me. Next to me lay my boyfriend and husband-to-be. We were catching our breath after making out in the dark on the hillside overlooking the sea with only the rainbow eucalyptus trees as our audience. Maybe, I thought at that moment, our relationship was a *thing*.

"How the hell did this relationship happen?" I wondered, not for the first time, snuggling closer.

Several months earlier, I had been going through my emails and website contact form submissions. One, in particular, had caught my eye. It read, "Hello, I don't know if you remember me, but we met a year ago in Fort Lauderdale at a meditation group. I just signed up for your Personal Mastery program." The email ended with his name, Adam Lamb.

"Fort Lauderdale?" I thought to myself, trying to place the encounter.

It took me a couple of minutes, but then it came back to me. "Oh, now I remember." I groaned at the computer screen. "He asked the question about love."

At the time I was with my boyfriend, Marco. We led meditation sessions in the area to generate interest for trips to the Bahamas. We took small groups of people to the islands to swim with the wild dolphins.

In the end, my relationship with Marco had ended badly. Deep in mourning and heartache, I began to doubt myself and the love that I once thought possible. It was a period of painful contraction for me.

I wrote, "Of course I remember you." During the meditation session, his question had redirected the entire conversation of that day. After a few moments of silence in the room, I answered his question with the story of how my marriage to my former husband had ended, and I found the love I always knew was possible with Marco.

"You're the chef, right?" I continued writing to Adam. "I'm taking a group to the Bahamas in three months, and we need a chef. Would you like to come along?" It was a bizarre thing to ask, given that I knew very little about him. "After all, he could be a chef-stalker-serial-killer, couldn't he?" I asked myself and my higher levels, half-jokingly. Sitting quietly with my eyes closed, I lowered my hands into my lap. Breathing in deeply, I felt a spark of expansion in my chest.

"It's always a yes until it feels contractive," I reminded myself, "so let's see what exactly is presenting." I hit send on the email.

I remain so grateful that Marco introduced me to the Bahamas and to the magic of swimming with the dolphins. After our relationship ended, the island still called to me, and I knew that I had to go back, this time without him. I sent him several emails, letting him know that to complete the circle with the painful events of our breakup and create my own relationship with the dolphins, island, and wonderful people there, I needed to come back with my own group.

He didn't like that at all. But my heart so clearly said that I needed to do that.

Adam's email reply came within hours. "Why, yes, I am a chef. I currently work in Tortola, BVI, so the Bahamas is a quick plane ride. I'm flattered that you remember me, considering it's been over a year since we met. I'd be happy to send you some menus; then, we can discuss a proposal and hopefully come to terms."

After a few more emails, we started to speak by phone to clarify the menus and the expectations. Then the calls got longer, and we started to discover more about each other. This was getting intriguing, but considering the pain of my recent relationships, I decided to keep the conversation loose and playful.

This whole situation with Adam made no sense. My feelings for him were deepening, despite my caution. I kept checking in with my body and my higher levels. The expansion in my chest felt even larger now, and that sensation was now accompanied by a force pulling me forward into my future.

I quickly consulted the list that described my perfect relationship in my head. Adam checked almost none of the boxes on the list. He had been married and divorced three times, had three children, and had experience with drugs and alcohol. He smoked. He listened to music I could only describe as sounding like a cat in a blender. He lived in the Caribbean. I lived in Canada.

"How could this ever work out?" the little me reasoned. "We'd better be very careful, or we'll get hurt again."

"The answer is still a yes," I reminded her, "so we continue until we get contraction."

The next time Adam and I spoke by phone, I decided to go all in and see what answer I got from the Universe. When there was a lull in the conversation, I said to Adam, "I think there's something else going on here, but I can't name it."

"You mean that we're falling in love with each other?" he replied instantly.

I feigned protest. "Listen, I'm Canadian; we don't just come out and say things like that." We laughed, but there it was, finally out in the open.

We met in Fort Lauderdale several weeks later, and it was electric on our way to the Bahamas. Three months of slowly developing our connection had led to this moment. Instead of being hesitant and clumsy around one another, we fell into each other's arms as if we were familiar companions.

Later we shopped for food for the trip, laughing our way through Whole Foods like kids on a treasure hunt. The preparation for the trip was light, playful, and healing for me.

The week in the Bahamas was blissful. Adam was amazing in the kitchen; everyone enjoyed his creativity and lively personality. More than once, I thought to myself, "I could really get used to this." His attention to detail and being in service to the clients was refreshing, and our skill sets seemed perfectly complementary. We made out a lot on that trip.

At the end of the week, Adam asked me, "Okay, now what?" I knew what he meant. After such an amazing experience being together, where do we go from here? Despite everything, I was still a little wary about getting hurt again.

"Well," I began, "I'll be in Maui in a month. A couple has lent me their house to finish my book." He leaned forward, close to my face. "You can meet me there."

A couple of days later, as I settled back home in Canada, I got an email from Adam.

It read: "Jennifer, I'll see you in Maui. I told my bosses here that I wouldn't be renewing my contract at the end of my term, and they've given me ten days to come to Hawaii. They told me they were sorry to see me go and asked if I had another offer. I told them no, this wasn't about another job. I told them that my heart was calling me forward, and even though I had no idea what that looked like, I would follow my heart's calling. I was going to follow my 'yes.'"

Then I saw it: at the bottom of the letter, he signed it, "ur man."

"Oh my," I thought to myself, "this really might be a thing."

I will also follow my yes and see just how far I can go before I get a number

We're married now, and we have a house and a dog. So far, so good.

The Ingredients for Living with You and Your Guidance as One

What we're saying is that you have 37 trillion cells that are directly connected to Infinite Wisdom. So much of your make-up is connected to every single dimension, and all the aspects of you that tie you back to all those other dimensions are also interconnected.

You don't need to excavate what you perceive to be in your way so you'll have the courage to go direct. That's kind of like saying you'd like to be an Olympic hurdler, but you're really scared of trying hurdling. If you could just get past being scared of trying hurdling, you'd be an expert hurdler, right? Well, that's a load of hooey, isn't it? The reason you're not an Olympic hurdler is that you haven't done any practice and you haven't even used the necessary muscles. And if someone taught you how to hurdle, and then you practiced over and over and over again, you'd become a pretty great hurdler. Even if you're seventy years old, you could still do it. That's all that's required.

I mean, how fun does life get when we go direct with Consciousness?

Going on this journey with Adam has been Olympic-level training in experiencing myself and my guidance as one. None of it made sense, but more often than not, doing what Life is presenting you isn't logical. It's an 'or better.'

The bottom line is that you're already going direct with Consciousness. You do things all the time because they feel expansive. Your body is alive because you're going direct. You make irrational right turns to avoid traffic because you're going direct. You know when your kids are up to something sketchy because you're going direct. This is just upping your game and applying that ability to all areas of life.

Action Steps

We have movie homework for you today.

The Adjustment Bureau.

This one will help get your brain ticking over on the subject of following your instincts and doing what life presents instead of giving your power away, even to your higher levels. You've got this. You have 37 trillion cells, and you get that you're in a dance with them. The only reason your higher levels exist, I swear to you, is so they can dance with you. They have no other job. They are yours, and you are theirs. You are intricately woven into this artwork, and the dance is part of the moving art of it all.

Blow it apart.

Have fun!

CHAPTER 9

DANCE WITH ANYTHING, WITHOUT BEING TAKEN OUT BY DISTRACTIONS, JUDGMENT, OR OVERWHELM

"Those who flow as life flows, know they need no other force."
Lao Tzu

What if you could engage anyone, or anything, from any time, space, or perspective without being taken out by your need to control or to be safe? What if nothing triggered you? What if you could be present to what's going on around you and stay neutral enough to know what to do?

Magical, right?

The Brain Bridge we're going to go through in this chapter is about going from feeling the need to control your life to learning the skills to enjoy or lean into every aspect of life while finding deliciousness in the process. That kind of confidence transcends the need to control and live predictably because life becomes so juicy that control becomes uninteresting. Paradoxically, being **UNSTUCK** requires that you don't control anything; you simply learn to dance with it all.

First, let's build an understanding of the meaning of being able to "dance with it all." Let's start with what *not* dancing with everything looks like.

Say you're at a party—maybe a community fundraiser for a homeless shelter. You're having a great conversation with an intelligent leader and all of a sudden someone joins your duo, and you become a trio. The third person is extremely opinionated about the homelessness issue in your town, and you feel like the entire conversation is being hijacked and is no longer constructive. You might get slightly triggered, fight back, try to convince the third person to take on your point of view, or leave. That's wrestling with it all, not dancing.

Another example of not dancing with it all happens all day, every day for most people. I'm sure it won't take a lot of imagination for you to come up with a project or opportunity that you judge makes absolutely no sense.

I remember a client who once told me about a huge real estate deal that she was doing with someone overseas who had all sorts of demands. She said it was too much for her, and I let her know that nothing happens *to* us; it only happens *for* us.

Her mind was already judging all the ways that it could go off the rails and thinking that she was only going to mess it up. She didn't know international real estate law or how to work with agents in that country, and she had collected evidence for everything that was going to go wrong.

She wasn't even willing to consider, let alone dance with, that opportunity because she had trained herself to operate from the idea that if it didn't make financial or business sense, she shouldn't do it.

By staying in the flow and being magnetic to the perfect people, she not only made more money than she had ever made but she also, more importantly to me, met her soul mate.

I have so many examples of clients who met their soulmates because they were following a passion project or a dream that put them into resonance with themselves. I had one client who was using the Thriving Operating System and voilà, a true soulmate showed up who didn't check any of the societal boxes yet entirely melted her heart.

That happened to me too!

I love nonlinear results. Why? Because nonlinear results are really quantum leaps, and as you know, I have an affinity for efficiency.

If you don't have a way to dance with everything and everyone that presents—even if it's just for clarity or a small "aha," or it's the opportunity to meet one person out of the one hundred people in the room—there's a degree of alchemy in life that's passing you by.

Here are some steps to optimize your ability to dance with it all when a new situation, person, or opportunity comes into your experience:

- Be curious about it.
- Know that it's happening for you, even if your personality doesn't like it.
- Ask yourself: Is this in front of me to engage with it? Am I supposed to get clarity about something from it? Can I assist the person or situation, and does that feel expansive? Or is this redirecting me somewhere else? Is it contractive, and do I know that something else is likely right up my alley?

The key is to approach the situation or person without adding your judgments and assessments. If it's happening for you, then there's nothing to protect yourself from. Again, be curious.

It might take a minute or a year to complete the steps, but if you continue dancing with it all, miracles start to become normal.

Buckminster Fuller said that these opportunities are part of the idea of precession, which is terminology usually related to gyroscopes; however, I'll use the analogy of a bee.[8] According to Fuller, new ideas, benefits, and opportunities will come every time two or more realities come together and act upon each other. The analogy often used is the idea of a honeybee not intending to benefit a flower that goes and does its job. It collects pollen on its body as a consequence. As a direct and unintended result, flowers cross-pollinate and produce fruit. Human beings, through their creativity, do the same when they do what Life is calling them to.

The beauty of knowing about precession is that once you're aware that the "energy" of any situation can change (in fact, it's designed to change) or that new opportunities can present, you can get curious about the situation, person, or opportunity in front of you instead of being protective.

Unstuckness requires that we stay in our expansive flow when we're interrupted by someone who is committed to arguing about a past or current situation. Also, unstuckness requires a new perspective on the paradigm of being in relationship to others.

---

8 Buckminster Fuller, Buckminster Fuller's Universe (New York: Basic Books, 1989), 93–95.

Allow me to share about a significant time when I said yes to something even though my logical mind screamed "no". This is about following the "yes" of life and distinguishing it from the "no" of your fears and doubts. I wouldn't be writing this book if I hadn't danced with this beautiful opportunity that was presented.

But I Really Don't Feel Like Doing This

I had been interviewed for a book called *Millionaire Women, Millionaire You* by my friend Stephanie J. Hale. There were several other successful women mentioned in the book, so Stephanie decided to create an event in London, England, where we would all come to speak. She called it the Millionaire Women's Bootcamp.

At this point in my career, I had either been paid for most of the speaking I did or I was speaking at programs I was teaching. Much of my speaking was for corporate clients. Stephanie's event was based on an idea called "speak to sell," a concept that is pervasive in the personal growth and speaking industries. My personality didn't like the idea of doing an hour-and-a-half sales pitch. "Yuck," said my personality.

Plus, hotels in London near the event were five hundred dollars per night.

Plus, I couldn't drive there on the other side of the road.

Plus, I wasn't going to know anyone there apart from Stephanie.

Plus, the videos I watched about how to speak to sell were filled with interesting mind-bending techniques that people work years to master. I had not mastered them. I could lose tens of thousands of dollars on the trip.

And my personality said, "Then I guess going to England is a number" Seemed logical. My thinking was probably logical to most people. Stephanie kept emailing me, I continued to see myself on that stage, and my physical body was filled with expansive "yes-ness" every time I thought about it.

Okay, now I will prepare you for the paradigm shift I experienced.

Most people live their lives to either avoid the past or prevent a future that reminds them of the past. Either way, the laws of physics say that you're going to recreate exactly what you don't want because it's included in the energy of what you're creating. So, you'll keep creating the past over and over again.

That is going round in circles. You've done it. I've done it. And it's not fun.

In this situation, my personality wanted to stay in a nice, safe circle. But my cells were feeling the call of the future that I had set into motion by being so passionate about what I do, helping lots of people, being interviewed for a book, and then being asked to speak about what I had said in the book.

The result was this: I decided to go and speak at the event. I met people in that audience who are still dear clients and friends. We then taught in Italy, Ireland, and Germany as a result. I also got to teach at an amazing Sufi center in London, England, wear the (very heavy) dress they wear, and learn about that culture, which led to doing a class with Sufis. And without using the "speak to sell" techniques, I sold more than most other speakers. I also ended up speaking at an event for women in Slovakia because a friend of the organizer really enjoyed our workshops. I later met some of the most beautiful human beings and broadened my inspiration to assist people so much more.

Anyone can move from a circular life to a spiral life—remember the geometry that the entire Universe is based on? And if you're able to dance with anything while doing what Life is presenting you while remaining curious instead of reactive, well, now you're onto something! The nature of civilization, our environment, and the Universe in which it all resides is continuously catalyzing or being catalyzed by other people, objects, and opportunities. So, when you master your ability to dance with what presents, it will move you into harmony with the way nature and the cosmos work. Wrestling keeps you in a never-ending loop of the past.

From this new level of understanding Life's design, we can experience synergy, flow, and thriving. Nothing was ever meant to stand still. If you avoid dancing with it all, you're avoiding opportunities that life is putting in front of you directly as a result of where you have been to be able to up-level or fast-track in some way. And if you were not a magnetic match to what Life is presenting you, then it would not have presented in the first place. Figuring out how—like I had to with that London event—happens in precession too, but you have to say yes first without knowing the how.

What comes to you is a direct result of what you've been nurturing and catalyzing by saying yes to the last thing you did or the last person you met.

Can you see why I keep inviting you to be curious on the adventure? Unless you aren't interested in thriving, of course. I do know it can sound scary to the part of you that wants control. The greatest control you'll ever have is when you're in sync with the entire Universe, driving the Ferrari of your life, with access to the gas, the brakes, and even the opportunity to park if you want.

And to be clear, this works in families, small businesses, big businesses, and dating. It isn't necessarily about getting on stage and speaking. It's a way of being, an operating system that you can use anywhere to help you live "the most fulfilling life, with the least amount of effort and the greatest amount of meaning and abundance in all areas, while enjoying your unfolding life completely."

I said yes to something I had no idea how to do. And I did it anyway because Life put it in front of me. Either I—and by that, I mean the essence of me pouring through this body—am the Universe in a drop and I have access to everything I need, or I'm not. The evidence suggests that, for me and for our clients, we are drops. I say let it rain.

It's not about doing something to your body so that you can receive it. What my guidance has shown me is that the human body has wiring, based on our DNA structure, that has atrophied over millennia, rendering it latent in most of us who are alive in this time of great change. As discussed in previous chapters, it seems counterintuitive that what scientists currently term junk DNA—80 percent of our DNA—has no purpose. Of course, in recent scientific studies, we're being shown that junk DNA suggest a pathway to abilities that allow us to dance in other dimensions.[9]

What would happen if the corpus callosum—the white matter that bridges the two hemispheres of the brain—were more fully developed? Studies show that the corpus callosum

9 Tushar Chauhan, "Why Is the So-Called Junk DNA Important for Us?" Genetic Education, July 7, 2021, https://geneticeducation.co.in/why-is-the-so-called-junk-dna-important-for-us/.

is nine percent more developed in those that play the piano, for instance. The left and right sides of the brain are designed to communicate to each other through the corpus callosum, and the brain is plastic. That means it can change. A more developed corpus callosum allows us to learn more quickly, bring creative ideas into reality and communicate in a way that gets results more efficiently. This suggests that there are parts of our modern-day brain that are underutilized.

Scientists are starting to develop a new understanding of the brain and mind, mapping neuronal cells to other parts of the body, such as the heart, which has its own neuronal network and gravitational field. Some cells in the brain are now believed to be communicating with interdimensional planes of existence through the mind's eye, challenging the standard definition of the brain as the seat of consciousness.[10] Some interesting recent studies have suggested that our mind is not merely a construct of our brain—rather, it exists elsewhere than in our neurons, and our brain is connected to far more than what our current scientific understanding would have us believe.[11]

This allows us to differentiate between the mind that is connected to "the field" which exists as a metaphysical structure, and the brain that consists of patterns, habits, and history.

When we're connected to the infinite field, there is no judgment. When we're connected to our history or our brain, we are vigilant for more of the past, and we stand guard, ready to judge. Connection with the field gives you the confidence

---

10 Olivia Goldhill, "Scientists say your 'mind' isn't confined to your brain, or even your body," Quartz, December 24, 2016, https://qz.com/866352/scientists-say-your-mind-isnt-confined-to-your-brain-or-even-your-body/.

---

11   Steve Taylor, "Why the Mind Is More than the Brain," Psychology Today, January 18, 2017, https://www.psychologytoday.com/us/blog/out-the-darkness/201701/why-the-mind-is-more-the-brain.

to dance with anything, whereas connection with your history has you recreating the past over and over again—thriving or survival.

The Ingredients for Dancing with It All

Let's talk about the ingredients for dancing with it all.

First, you might consider developing an intolerance for struggle. Nature doesn't struggle; it simply lives directly in relation to its environment, integrating, growing, and shining forward. You're made of the same atoms that came from the ground that made a tree. You're wired to flourish. An intolerance for struggle without judgment will redirect your attention to the solutions that cause flow.

This leads to the next idea, which is about slowing down to speed up in this world. We're so wired to go, go, go. Ya gotta go, ya gotta accomplish, ya gotta get it all done, ya gotta make sure things are looked after. But if you don't slow down, you'll never be present to the space between the atoms where pure possibility lives or to the solutions that are birthed by the contrast you're living. Not to mention the opportunities that you can't see when you're too busy to be a good dance partner with your greater Consciousness.

The next ingredient is that you have to be willing to understand that most of what you think is just a well-practiced habit. Just because it's well practiced doesn't make it rock your world. We used to do an exercise where we encouraged people to ask themselves, "What is in the highest?" But the problem was that the question got them into their intellectual processing center. It had people thinking, not dancing. When you're dancing with it all, in mastery, there's very little overthinking because you're too busy creating.

Consider this: the Universe is in every atom. It doesn't just *have* your back; it *is* your back, in an interesting way. It's in the Universe's best interest to put in front of you that which would have you flourish, as Consciousness learns from your journey and expands based on your choices. It is having an experience through you while *you* have an experience through *it*. Hence, it is holographic. If that's true, then what it puts in front of you on a moment-by-moment basis reflects the trajectory of thoughts and actions you've taken, telling it (as its dance partner) what you're interested in. You are a living intention in a dance with the Creative force that makes worlds. Engage with what life brings your way, with curiosity on the adventure, instead of fear on the uncontrollable carnival ride. You're being either affirmed or redirected. Either way, it's all moving you toward the fulfillment of the ultimate expression of your skills through this life because that's the most efficient way to create.

Action Steps

Have some fun with this.

We posted a clip from the Jim Carrey movie *Yes Man* on our *UNSTUCK* Action Plan page (https://thewideawakening. com/unstuckresources). It's a great movie, and you can watch all of it if you want. This clip might make you think, "Oh my God, I can't say yes to everything!" But the essence of the movie is that the main character is just doing what's right in front of him at each moment, and all kinds of miraculous things happen as a result.

You might laugh, and you might think it's a silly idea, but it's closer to how we're designed than strategizing, trying to get things right, and trying not to be judged while letting our identities run us.

The very act of being willing to engage with Consciousness is going to rewire you.

In fact, by doing things differently than you *have* done, you're telling All That Is that you're interested in changing things up. Already, your grip on old patterns is loosening, not because you directly changed them, but because you're considering and approaching life a little differently.

We look forward to helping you explore your options to become a member of the Heaven on Earth Construction Crew by visiting https://thewideawakening.com/ .

CHAPTER 10

FREEDOM FROM JUDGMENT OF YOURSELF AND OTHERS

*"People will judge you whether you
change yourself for them or not.
If you simply be yourself, however,
at least one of you is happy."*
J. Hough

What would happen if we relinquished the need or impulse to judge ourselves, or anyone else for that matter? How do we find that kind of courage? How free could we feel? Who else would be inspired? Wouldn't you like to find out?

At one time or another, all of us have been judged by parents, siblings, teachers, classmates, coworkers, lovers, or friends. At one time or another, we've all judged ourselves or someone else. Judgment seems to be a natural reaction for human beings. And yet it's not—creativity is our most natural state.

In this chapter, we'll go beyond judgment. Judgment is the product of a protective mechanism created by your personality to keep you from being a tall, radiant, ridiculously fulfilled poppy.

When you judge someone else, you're proactively protecting yourself from any hurt they might cause you. Your protective identities believe it's better to make someone else wrong than to be vulnerable about what's happening within you or around you.

Your protective identities are trying to save you from physical pain, or worse, death. They were developed through past experiences where you were hurt, judged, or scared.

"You can't give that presentation; you don't know enough."

"Lie low," your little voice says. "Don't be the tall poppy; they always get cut down."

Fun fact about judgment: you can judge the judgment. It sounds unfair. This is a little trick that your protective mechanisms use to ensure you never live fully as yourself, following your heart's calling.

In other words, the original judgment might be, "My body is fat; I have lumps everywhere." But then you catch yourself and go further down the rabbit hole. "Oh my God, I'm judging my lumps! I can't believe I'm judging my lumps! Look at me, that just guarantees that I'm going to be fat! I can't even get 'loving myself' right."

See how that works? You've just nailed the coffin lid of your self-esteem shut. Right now, you might be saying to yourself, "Jeez, I do that all the time, dammit, I suck." You've just won the "Triple Crown of Judging the Judgment" by using what I said to judge yourself a third time. Cut that out!

Have grace. Everyone does it. You're probably just trying to do your best in life, and someone told you that judgment and criticism would motivate you. Alas, that's not true. If a way of being doesn't feel expansive, then that's not a way of being that Life gave you so that you thrive; it's one that humans gave you so that you fit in.

So, what is the flawed paradigm in this way of thinking?

We got taught early on in life that getting it right is the aim and that if we do that, we'll be acceptable, lovable, or, at the very least, approved of.

This paradigm is pervasive in sports, schools, families, and businesses.

It's all about winning the survival game. Yikes, that's so second-best and unfulfilling. I know because I was pretty good at it myself.

The reason that judgment of self or others, or being judged, feels so awful or contractive is that we were never supposed to be guided by another's opinion of us in the first place! The whole paradigm is flawed.

We were meant to go directly with that expansive or contractive feeling that lets us know whether or not we're aligned with the future trajectory that is calling us. Period. End of story.

Your connection with Life, Greater Wisdom, or whatever you choose to call it is what was always meant to guide your existence.

Think of what others have to say as excellent input that you will consider and you may or may not let them know if you agree, but you appreciate their perspective and will run it through your wise, omnipotent guidance that has your back. If what they say, feel, or judge inspires you or is valuable, it will feel expansive to consider. If it's not, you'll need to ask for clarity if you feel you misunderstand what they are saying, or it's just contractive and therefore not something you want to take on because it isn't true for you.

End of story.

Now, what if we went back through your entire life and re-perceived every difficult event through that new paradigm of judgment? What would happen to the ideas you made up about yourself, life, and others?

The Universe doesn't judge a duck-billed platypus; it doesn't judge your lumps, it doesn't judge your height or the color of your eyes. Infinite Wisdom doesn't judge how anyone behaves toward someone else, no matter how horrific it might seem to you.

Think of the judgment of others as either "an affirmation of what is true" or "clarity about what is not true." Your essence is a filter, of sorts, to determine whether what is said feels expansive or contractive. Once you understand that, there is no need to take things personally. The clarity either way is doing you a favor.

And you can start doing that today.

In human terms, Creation is always asking, "How can we start from here and find more Heaven? How can we find more flow?" Judgment makes flow almost impossible.

This is where Jeannie Selda started, with a huge act of saying yes to something that her heart was calling her toward, despite her family, friends, and culture having something to say about it. Here is Jeannie's story, in her own words.

Selfish or Self-Full

I was born in Canada to Filipino parents. They thought it best that I return to the Philippines to be raised by my grandparents while they got established in their new home country. Five years later, I returned to Canada.

Growing up a "good" Filipina also meant being a good Catholic. I was encouraged to view all my efforts as a contribution to my family, and my own desires and needs were subordinated to those of my family, community, and church.

Jesus died for our sins, and if he could do it, then so should we. Personal martyrdom was seen as a pathway to redemption, and I was taught that this would ensure I'd have a seat closer to God's right hand when my time came.

I was taught that everyone came before me: my family, husband, children, and even job. Filipino families do everything together. The brothers, sisters, uncles, aunts, and cousins all get together to celebrate every secular and religious holiday, christening, and baptism with barbecues and house parties.

I remember being consumed with needing and seeking the approval of my husband, my parents, my friends, my employer...everyone! I was perfectly comfortable being the wind beneath everyone else's wings. I had to be the best at everything I did, which usually meant putting my needs last; that's how important someone else's approval, happiness, and comfort were to me.

Being so focused on everyone else meant that there was little room for any dream or aspiration of my own. At home, I hung up a poster of Machu Picchu with the silent hope that, one day, I would visit that mystical place. Something about the image spoke softly but insistently to me.

I had been working part time with Jennifer at her home office for a few months when she announced that The Wide Awakening was going to be taking a group of people to Peru to visit Machu Picchu. My heart leaped into my throat when I heard the news. I told her about my dream, saying, "I don't see how I could ever make that happen. My twins are only four years old, and how could I possibly take a trip without them?"

Could I leave my kids at home and go on this wild adventure by myself? What would my husband and family say? As soon as I said it, I knew what some of my family members would say. I resigned to the likelihood that going to Peru was just a pipe dream.

Jennifer replied, "Jeannie, you could always put down a deposit, say one hundred dollars, to hold your spot. If you don't end up going, I'll give you your deposit back."

That sounded reasonable to me, even though I had no idea where the other $3,900 would come from. I wrote the check and handed her the deposit. She told me to keep moving energy in the direction of my "yes" and just relinquish judgment for the time being.

That night, after putting the boys to bed, I told my husband about what had transpired at the office. "Jeannie, I never knew you wanted to go to Peru," Andrew said. He continued, "I just don't know how we'd swing it financially."

That seemed to be the end of the conversation, yet my heart started to lift. Just thinking of the possibility that I might go kept me energized. As I worked on the details of the trip and the participants, I found myself imagining more and more about what it would be like to step foot on that ancient plateau. I wasn't thinking about whether I would or wouldn't go; I just went on the journey in my mind and my heart. It felt great, even though I knew that some family members would think I'd abandoned my good Catholic girl status, willfully ignoring the original commandment, "Put thyself last, just like Jesus did."

About a month later, I checked our lottery tickets in the local pharmacy. My heart stopped when I realized that we had just won $5,000.

I called Andrew and said, "Babe, I have some good news and some bad news."

"Go on," he said.

"Well, the good news is that we won $5,000. The bad news is that it was your ticket, not mine. LOL!"

That night when I got home from work, he asked me to sit down. "Honey, I know how much the trip to Peru means to you," he began. "Give me a grand from the winnings, and you keep the rest of the money for the trip. The family and I can look after the boys while you're gone."

I jumped up from my chair, and even though things hadn't been going well in the marriage, I threw my arms around him, feeling incredibly grateful for him. "Thank you, thank you, thank you!" I started to cry at the thought that my dream was about to come true.

After changing planes three times, we finally landed in Cusco, Peru. We then rode three hours in a caravan into the Sacred Valley and our resort, Willka T'ika. After checking in, we all gathered in the beautiful, huge yoga room overlooking the mountains. As everyone left for their rooms, I decided to stay behind and do some stretching to work out some travel kinks. It was there, as I was sitting alone on my mat and looking out on the Sacred Valley bathed in the sunset, that the enormity of what was happening struck me, and I began to sob.

Soon I was in a complete emotional breakdown, crying heavily, my chest heaving, as I remembered the journey to get there. It felt like every protective mechanism that had ever kept me safe was blowing up inside me, and there was no way to stop it.

All the expectations, conditioning, and stories from my culture and religion that I had taken on fell away from me. All the hopes, dreams, and aspirations for my life that I had locked away in my heart came back, flowing through me.

As my breathing slowed and I returned to the present, I heard someone say, "Welcome home, Jeannie. Welcome back to your heart."

That night I slept soundly, finally free of all the identities I had willingly taken on. The next morning, I was more than ready for our hike up to Machu Picchu.

Self-Full It Is

I was so tickled that Jeannie decided to embrace who she is and make that more important than her judgments of herself or the judgments of others. She was immersed in a culture with very specific ideas about what motherhood should look like. She was immersed in a religion that venerated martyrdom. She had to be perfect at everything, sacrificing who she was in favor of her family. Suddenly she said, "I'm going to Peru for two weeks, and I'm leaving my young twin boys with their dad." Almost everyone in her family said, "You can't do that!"

Imagine the courage it took for her to turn her back on years of conditioning and finally say yes to her dream and, more importantly, herself. Yet her whole life has changed since then because she said yes. She has now worked with The Wide Awakening for fifteen years. She found her passion in photography, and some of her best pictures are from subsequent trips to Peru with us. Sometimes it just takes one act of following your heart to change the rest of your life.

She was defined by society's rules and roles being projected on her. Even though she was a "good mom, wife, mother, Catholic, Filipina," she was in disharmony, ignoring her piece of the puzzle of Heaven on Earth that she came here to be. Harmony and fulfillment can only happen when you're harmonized with your heart's true calling first. Jeannie told me later that her spirit is adventurous and doesn't want to be contained by identities, yet that's what was happening.

To be free enough to become the best version of herself, including her roles as mother and partner, Jeannie was required to regain all of herself and to make decisions that were mutually honoring.

Luckily for us, she did. Now, Jeannie has changed and has shaken the trees of so many in her family, and she kicks my butt back to congruence all the time because she knows how important it is for The Wide Awakening. Her children are rock stars and find their own paths, just like she did. They both went from being reliant on her to being reliant on their own knowledge, and they're so awesomely confident as a result.

Sometimes, loving yourself first is exactly what love would do.

Heed the Call

When we take action on what is calling our heart, it's an act of mutual honoring. I thank William Linville for that phrase, as it has permeated my cells. In this case, mutual honoring is when Jeannie honored herself, her heart's calling, and her family by being an example of a human in integrity with her very nature.

It is an act of mutual honoring to do what love would do... for yourself as much as for others.

When you perceive that someone or society judges you, often you'll morph your behavior into something more acceptable to them, much like Jeannie did, and, for that matter, much like I did too. You voluntarily change your way of being to make someone else more comfortable. You might think, "My mother thinks that nothing I ever do is right, so I'm going to try to spend the rest of my life trying to be good enough."

If someone judges you and you change your behavior, you can guarantee that both of you will be miserable. The person who is judging you won't be happy because they're separating themselves from the entire Universe, choking off fulfillment and flow. No matter how you show up, it'll never be enough for them because you've trained them that you are interested in making them happy or unhappy. You may be good, but you're not *that* good, at least not yet! Once you change your behavior to make the other person feel less threatened, superior, or safe, you won't be expressing yourself fully. In doing so, you'll be less than the piece of the puzzle of Heaven on Earth that you came here to be, and finding meaning, fulfillment, and enjoyment in your life will be a struggle.

Can you see how contractive it is to play the game of avoiding judgment, hiding from judgment, trying to be perfect, and making societal judgments important? The real issue is about making judgments of others, or your well-practiced self-judgment that came from your own history, important. The only thing that matters is your own feeling of contraction or expansion regarding any subject. It's the quickest way to know whether or not you're in alignment.

Mutual honoring also means that when you follow your heart, you honor the whole. By you being who you are, in a fractal Universe, you give permission to others to stop morphing themselves because of the fear of judgment. Again, another aspect of true freedom.

The big question is this: will you be judged for following your heart and therefore Life's calling? Absolutely.

And will you be judged even if you follow society's version of who you should be? You betcha.

So, you might as well follow your heart's calling. At least one person in the equation will be happy.

That way, you get the bonuses of being fully self-expressed, teaching your kids to follow their heart, inspiring your friends, retraining the people around you about who you are, and leaving the door open for the possibility that some of your family members will find freedom.

When you decide to "fit out" instead of fitting in, you become a leader or inspiration of sorts. Don't worry, you don't need to carry that—it's not a cross, it's just what happens. When the judgments become noise in the background, there are no limits to how much you can experience and how much love you can emanate. There's no limit to how much you can contribute to someone else. And there's no limit to how much someone else can contribute to you.

In the flow of abundance, your only job is to be willing to enjoy it all. Becoming the piece of the puzzle of Heaven on Earth that you came here to be means fully expressing your creativity, joy, and brilliance regardless of anyone else's opinion or judgment about you. When you practice disentangling from the projections of others, not only will you be truly free to be all you really are, but in turn you free them to consider not judging who they are as well. You give them the gift of compassion, which might encourage them to evaluate for themselves whether judging others is a game they want to continue to play.

The iconic book *A Course in Miracles* says that everything someone does is either an act of love or a cry for love.[12] It's clear which category judgment falls into.

You might be feeling heard, and you might start to feel understood. You might even be tempted to understand a bit more compassionately.

It may serve you to know that it has nothing to do with you when anyone judges you. It's always and forever about fear of the unknown and the instinct to protect against the unpredictable. From that perspective, how might you react to their judgment?

Ingredients for Having Freedom around Judgment in All Forms

Years ago, I coordinated a barn-raising for a friend. It was at a beautiful horse farm with a great event space in the woods. But it was falling apart because of a legal suit from a suboptimal neighbor who was the very skeptical husband of one of the women helping at the farm (she lodge1d her horse there). He must have been in the banking industry!

He saw fit to harass me, saying that soon everyone would find out that I was doing it for my own gain. Of course I was not—the owners were dear friends, and I just wanted to help. His emails were nasty and relentless.

I started to engage him and tried to convince him he was wrong. Sometimes we do that when we have a self-judgment

---

12 Helen Schucman and William Thetford, eds., A Course in Miracles (New York: Foundation for Inner Peace, 1975).

that sounds like what our critic is saying. Not a good idea because all it does is amplify the issue.

A powerful phrase that I often use now to make sure family, friends, and colleagues feel heard while I still get to honor myself is this: "I don't see it that way, but I honor how you feel about it." Judgment has now been replaced with neutrality. You've just allowed your partner, boss, or competitor the right to their own feelings without invalidating yours. A world of possibilities has opened up for both of you.

I wish I had known about that phrase then. Ugh. The drama would have lasted for much less than two months.

I share this because that man's skepticism about goodness in the world was not mine to carry. I actually spent time trying to convince him that there were good people out there.

This is not the time to worry about the judgments of others—it's time to get moving and change the world around those people. Let's change the world around them so much that they no longer live separate from themselves and those around them. This is a great act of love.

Disentangle from judgment. Instead, let the negativity catalyze you to clarify what you want more of in the world. You have the privilege of leading the way to a new and deeper understanding. It's going to require that you stand up for yourself. Do it in a way that expresses compassion and understanding. Don't jeopardize your ability to fly forward by being righteous. The people you're meant to affect won't be swayed by anything else but humility.

Remember that those who judge you, including yourself, are simply afraid and are distracting themselves from their fear by not minding their own business. What do you do when you know someone is afraid instead of judging them as judgmental?

Don't get caught spending all your time and energy on defending yourself.

All are worthy of your love, but in a body, on a planet, we have only so much time, so be discerning about who you give your time and attention to.

Action Steps

This week, consider using this statement: "I totally understand how you could feel that way. It's not how I feel, but I honor where you are."

A very productive set of words that can save you lots of drama!

CHAPTER 11

YOUR SUPERPOWERS

"Whoever you think you are, you are."
Dr. Joe Dispenza

What if we are all gifted? We just haven't realized the gifts yet, and if we had, life would get a lot easier.

To create like a pro, we need to bring our heavenly, metaphysical, beyond reason, subatomically accessible wisdom and superpowers through this body in 3D so that we can experience the bliss of being the creators of our realities and experience what is possible on this heavenly planet.

We were not meant to ascend; we were meant to descend from the space between atoms, the quantum field, those superpowers into our bodies by using them fully.

Being ethereal and trying to get to the promised land by winning the enlightenment Olympics (no, there is no such thing, my dear friend William Linville made that up) doesn't help the CEO of a Fortune 500 company I just worked with. And it doesn't help the naturopath I worked with who is building bridges to end autoimmunity. Finally, it does not help my new friends who are changing the face of healthcare (like Dr. Dorothy Martin-Neville), empowering young people (like Dr. Valerie Sheppard), and revolutionizing the education system (like Natalie Ledwell) globally from the inside out in brilliant ways.

One must 'descend' (from the field) or embody the ability to connect consistently to clarity and guidance. One must remember how to connect with others heart to heart to build bridges of understanding of ourselves first and others; one must reclaim one's greater abilities to create, reimagine, and build new realities to be a part of the world we desire. One must tell deeper truths relentlessly and build mutually honoring systems.

It is time to come alive with the fulfillment and meaning that are birthed from experiencing our lives through all of our abilities, not just the ones that help us merely survive.

Some call this 5D or activating the crystalline grid. Again, not helpful for the regular person, although fairly accurate. Of course, we can use that language if we wish. It's just that *everyone* was meant to be included in thriving. Everyone has superpowers.

These days, it is pretty clear that many simply want to argue about the existing problems, which are based on straight-up laws of physics and biophysics, but arguing only recreates the reality you have.

Cosmic Lavender

As my friend Steffny Wallace reads this section title "Cosmic Lavender," she will cringe, I suspect. She calls her lavender enlivened because it is.

Her essence and passion enliven it. And it is also enlivened by the azeztulite she saw was necessary to bring certain characteristics to the lavender she planted.

Steffny's story is amazing. She is a television producer and became a dear friend through the process of being in our advanced program, Flight School. She was already deeply guided by her Greater Wisdom before I met her, yet there were areas of her life that 'could be better,' to use her words.

Having visited Steffny's lavender farm many times, Running Springs Ranch, as many do because it is also a gorgeous glamping area, I have to say that there is magic in the air.

As Steffny's story goes, long before anyone had even said the word lavender, she had started having awakened dreams. She was shown a way to amplify peace, love, and tranquility on the planet in a way she had never considered before. She became an even clearer channel of information that, in these days of such polarity, is profoundly effective in helping people find their center and relax. To this day, I know she still receives messages to evolve her highly unique farming and extraction techniques. I am not surprised that someone who has been in such a dog-eat-dog industry for most of her life was catalyzed by guidance to create a way to find the peace that can be helpful to all.

Steffny is a shining example of what is possible when we awaken to our Innate Abilities. Her full story is at www.RunningSpringsRanch.com. It's worth reading if you are interested in what Superpowers look like.

I'm sure we'll be teaching a course on Superpowers in her event space soon.

Steffny's story is not only about her superpowers; it's a powerful reminder that we have resources available to us that are beyond reason.

Are you ready to come home to your superpowers?

The rest of this chapter takes a deviation from the other chapters. You are invited to join me on video! We'll explore the Innate Abilities—the superpowers—you and your fellow humans have. You'll learn activations and tools to awaken and remember these abilities.

Action Steps

This chapter is so important to me that I knew that I needed to do it on video for you. There are so many drawings and illustrations that can be used that we decided to create a bonus video chapter.

You can get it here:

https://thewideawakening.com/unstuckresources.

CHAPTER 12

ENDING SELF-SABOTAGE

*"The issue is not the issue; that you
made it the issue is the issue."*
J. Hough

This chapter is not about judgment, which we covered previously—although judgment does play a part in self-sabotage. In a quiet, subversive way, self-sabotage starts with self-judgment. That same judgment, which is embodied as a thought, repeated over time, becomes a belief through which we sabotage ourselves from our highest and most fulfilling path.

We project forward into the future how our life could be, or more accurately, how our new life should be different from our past experiences. In our minds, we often construct a possible future based on the image of how we think things should be at the expense of acknowledging what's going on. Or we project a future that corrects the past, which, based on the laws of physics, will only put the past in our future yet again.

While we're engaged in such emotional time travel, either projecting our past into the future or mentally rehearsing our future despite our history, at no time are we present to All That Is at this moment, the only place where the magic occurs.

Here's an example. I used to be scared to bring up controversial subjects with my ex. My previous experience with men was not pleasant when it came to difficult conversations, and they ended in a lot of yelling. Instead of dealing with the energy in front of me with my ex, I would defend myself, even though there was no attack going on in the present moment. That would only make my ex more frustrated. Hence, I was totally sabotaging the awesome conversation that could have been.

If you see yourself in the description above, don't let it take you out of the journey of discovery that this chapter promises.

Put simply, we all sabotage ourselves. Or do we?

Here's a thought: what if, from a higher point of view, self-sabotage is simply not being ready yet for the next evolution—vibrationally, three-dimensionally, or emotionally? What if it's more of a calling to shift our perspective and skills than a reason to beat ourselves up?

Self-Sabotage as Carrying versus Caring

Sometimes self-sabotage expresses itself differently. We may be trying to convince ourselves that we're acting out of love and compassion for someone else—carrying them instead of caring for them. It's a subtle distinction but one worth clarifying.

At its highest, caring for a child might look like giving them a deadline for moving out of your house and then going with them to look at apartments. Carrying them might feel like they'll never be able to stand on their own, so you renovate the basement. Now, they have their apartment rent-free.

As we've mentioned a few times, carrying another is a form of sabotage for you, as the energy you spend carrying someone is not spent on your own dreams and goals. It's also spiritually arrogant to think that the wisdom that comes through your body, based on your experience, would necessarily apply to someone else's experience as deeply as it did to yours.

The wisdom that someone else needs will be according to their past, struggles, and experience. That's why couples often go around in circles with the same issues all the time.

Let's have grace here. The reason we offer advice to another, at least at the outset, is because we care (and sometimes carry) their upset.

Consider that more often than not, it's your own discomfort with someone else's situation that makes you offer them advice. That's not really about them though. Just saying.

Another question. Are we in our own way? Or are we in Creation's way? Or—because we are so intimate with Creation—are we in the way of the future possibility that we launched through our dreams, goals, and prayers?

What if, through the very use of the terminology "self-sabotage," we're actually making it easy for the "little me" to judge ourselves and distract us from doing the things we need to do to upgrade ourselves to the level of the dreams we have?

Tolerance

Throughout this book, I've tried to be as precise as possible and use the most accurate words each topic will permit. That can be difficult because so many words have several different meanings with other connotations depending on the context in which they're used. Words have power and consequences, so I've tried to use them wisely and accurately.

Permit me to split one more hair. I'd like to reference a word that hasn't appeared in this book so far. The word is tolerance. It applies to other chapters too, but I want to examine its implications within the context of self-sabotage.

The Merriam-Webster dictionary defines the word tolerance as:

1. The capacity to endure pain or hardship: endurance, fortitude, stamina.
2. Sympathy or indulgence for beliefs or practices different from or conflicting with one's own.
3. The act of allowing something: toleration.
4. The allowable deviation from a standard.
5. The capacity of the body to endure or become less responsive.
6. The relative ability to grow or thrive when subjected to an unfavorable environmental factor.

Well, your cells can tolerate only so much judgment and distraction before the dissonance between what your heart is calling you toward and what is happening ends in symptoms, chronic issues, and then acute issues if you haven't been listening. So emotional self-sabotage can result in physical symptoms that drive it home.

And yes, you can often find a way to heal simply by addressing what you didn't address originally.

Unfortunately, we sometimes confuse tolerance with tenacity. Is it really in the highest good for your life to tenaciously pursue projects and relationships that aren't working? Society values tenacity, but that's unfortunate in cases such as abusive relationships. However, I think it would serve us to examine what we tolerate when we're discussing self-sabotage.

Merriam-Webster's definition of the word doesn't explicitly say this, but in my experience, anyone who tolerates anything usually does so against their better judgment.

My husband Adam seems to enjoy difficult conversations.

Instigating drama becomes a convenient way to mitigate risk and kick the can of the inevitable decision or action down the road for a few more months.

And that's yet another form of self-sabotage. In the past, Adam tolerated not moving through issues quickly because he judged himself so badly that he made every hard discussion about himself. Those discussions felt so awful to him that putting them off was more tolerable than living with the pain of not addressing the self-sabotaging habit. Which in itself is self-sabotaging. Or so it would seem.

It serves us to pay attention to these little heart whispers, the discomfort in our bodies, and the contraction of our spirit.

It's not that we are tolerating self-judgment or struggle. It's that we are tolerating *not* being attuned to the heart's whispers because if we were, self-sabotage wouldn't happen. We would address things as they came up. We would have the conversations that needed to be had. We would do things in perfect divine timing instead of our personality's timing.

One detail that we often ignore in calculating the emotional cost of tolerance is that it comes with an expiration date. Your body starts having symptoms to let you know! Remember that your body never lies to you, and when you're off track in your thinking, beliefs, or paradigms, you'll start with little things like a stiff neck, a sore back, or headaches, and you'll go from there.

When the clock of tolerance finally runs out and you feel frustrated about being taken advantage of, you might decide that more drastic action is needed to get your point across, when intolerance to symptoms and the heart's whispers would have had you addressing the issue long ago.

In the flush that comes after an unfortunate confrontation, you might very well judge yourself harshly, kicking your ass around the corner and back again. "How could a good person do something like that?" you ask yourself. "There must be something wrong with me." And so you continue the cycle of self-sabotage.

What is the antidote to tolerance? It's neutrality, and if you're really courageous, you'll develop a serious intolerance to incongruence within yourself and have the discussions that need to be had. Those kinds of discussions are always best held when you're open to letting love win.

The Third Entity

Traditional mathematics state that $1 + 1 = 2$ is a fact that is as unalterable as the sun. But quantum mechanics and theoretical physicists suggest that when two come together, there is a third entity birthed that equals the entity that gets created from that new relationship. Therefore $1+1=3$.

At The Wide Awakening, we have embraced this concept of the "third entity". I've seen it at work in my relationship with my sweetie, Adam.

With all my history, faults, and insecurities, there's the little me. Over there is my sweetie with all his baggage, his self-protective mechanisms, and his cat-in-a-blender musical tastes. Sigh, nothing about him checked any of the boxes on my special list, but there you go…sometimes magic makes no sense.

When we came together, energetically, and emotionally, that union created a third entity that we called Jennifer and Adam together in the Quantum Field, and it became a portal through which we could connect with Infinite Wisdom and every possibility that exists for our relationship. There is only love, compassion, and grace in the third entity, and it is devoid of protective mechanisms, fear, or lack.

There is no such thing as self-sabotage. There's only "What can we do now to create?"

Letting Love Win

In the early days, whenever we got caught up in an emotional struggle, often initiated by the magnetism of our "pain point" or "quantum entanglement," we would stop and consider, "What would Love do?" or "How can we let Love win?"

Sometimes that looked like willingness to let the other person take a few minutes to ground themselves. Often it looked like beholding each other from that higher perspective where there is no need to judge, because the Universe never judges, it only asks the question, "From this vantage point, how can we emanate more love?"

I'm not going to say that it was easy at first. To succeed, it first required a level of self-awareness that we didn't have. Being committed to our relationship and the flawed individuals it encompassed meant that sometimes we couldn't continue until we first got into our hearts. That generally required going for a walk in nature, watching a funny movie, talking with a friend we love, or going to the gym and listening to some inspirational music.

More About Third Entities

In her book *Big Magic*, Elizabeth Gilbert writes that she believes that ideas that give rise to artistic endeavors float around as disembodied entities, yearning to be brought forth into reality.[13]

These potentialities—and I'm paraphrasing right now—float along until they resonate with and are attracted to an equivalent frequency of desire from an author looking for their next bestseller. Someone's gotta want it, after all.

This potential piece of perfection wants to flourish forward with someone who is lined up with the creation of the dream that is wanting to be.

It's then that the idea joins the author in the Quantum Field. In the portal created by the third entity of them joining forces and committing to a certain outcome, a narrative is passed into the writer's mind from the potentiality. The idea says to the author, "If you're going to enjoy the milk, partner, then you'll have to buy the whole cow. Let's rock this."

An idea, eager to become real, comes with an expectation of expediency. It has spent plenty of time searching for the most efficient partner, so there's only so long it'll hang around, waiting for the author to set about their work.

If in good time the author is still diddling around with the acknowledgments, then the disembodied entity will pack its bag and hit the road to look for the next most likely person to bring it to fruition.

That's why multiple authors can have the same book idea at the same time. For one reason or another, all the others have given up the chase, and the potentiality, seeking fulfillment, will continue pursuing the one who's willing to go the distance and put in the work, love, and dedication required to birth the idea into the world for all to enjoy.

13 Elizabeth Gilbert, Big Magic: Creative Living Beyond Fear (New York: Riverhead Books, 2015).

Creation experiencing itself through its creation is a perfect example of the third entity and the opportunity to transcend self-sabotage.

The third entity needs to be nurtured, cared for, and tended with love. That requires a presence to appreciate what that relationship, idea, or dream provides to our lives. If the third entity isn't nurtured, the portal closes and moves on to find someone else willing to meet it in the place where all possibilities exist. And that could be you if you're ready to suspend your beliefs and double down on faith.

If we don't acknowledge the unique nature of our relationship to dreams, people, projects, and the third entity that gets created as a result (so cool), the lack of acknowledgment and, therefore, lack of attention is a form of "self-sabotage." Another issue in all honesty, is that we have to become aware that there is a third entity that needs attention in the first place. So now you know!

Whatever you create from the dance between you and Infinite Wisdom becomes a third entity. These possibilities do not come from a collection of history, projections, or expectations from your parents, classmates, or lovers.

Most of us have minimal experience or practice with the third entity created from the dance between you and All That Is.

Know that the subtleties of dancing with that greater knowing take practice.

Are We Really Ever Self-Sabotaging, Or…?

Consider that if you want to thrive, you aren't ever really sabotaging yourself, you're only unpracticed at creating what's next. It makes sense since most dreams are things you've never

done before. So, are you sabotaging yourself? Or are you just giving yourself a breather so that you can get the information you need, find the necessary resources, and search for the people who can make it easier?

Earlier, we talked about judging the judgment. What if we removed the concept of self-sabotage altogether?

What if, in a universal sense, there's no reason for calling it self-sabotage because all that's really happening is that you haven't caught up with the answers or skills you need for what's next?

Maybe all there is to do is ask for help, get trained, or look for ideas.

How do we bring it forth as a tangible thing into our third dimension without having a clear idea of it or what it wants to become?

The "little you" loves to hold on to a predictable outcome; that way, it can calculate what might happen based on the most reliable prognostication and then fashion a strategy for dealing safely with each possible consequence. The "little you" is not a fan of uncertainty or having too many variables in the equation.

But for a life that is fulfilling, meaningful, abundant, and expanding forward at the speed of your heart's calling, predictability is the booby prize.

Moving Past Self-Sabotage, a Story by Adam M. Lamb

I am out on the front porch smoking, pacing in the dark as this story is being written. I'm emotionally untethered and enjoying the dissonance much more than I should.

At this moment, there's a part of me that's convinced that, in this condition, I'm more than any two people can handle right now, at least not without a straitjacket, a shot of Librium, and an ambulance waiting in the driveway.

What can I say? As a writer, I'm given to bouts of hyperbole. It's cute at first, but the shine quickly wears thin without moderation.

It all started a month ago when Jennifer asked me to help her finish her book.

"A book?" I thought to myself, "I didn't know she was writing a book!"

"Okay, how long do we have?" I was stalling until I knew more about what I'd agreed to do. I had written several self-published books, so I understood the process well.

"Friday," she said over her shoulder as she headed out the door for a hike down by the river in the bamboo forest she loves. Jennifer is the only person I know who can find a tropical forest in the mountains of North Carolina.

"Friday?" I yelled after her. "It's Monday, and we're hosting a retreat all week!" "What the fu—" my voice trailed off as her car pulled out of the driveway.

"Okay, yeah, sure, why not?" I said to the only companion left on the porch, Mighty Mouse, our dog. I'm pretty sure that he couldn't care less then, as now, whether I ever wrote another word, just as long as he didn't have to wait for his breakfast.

As it turned out, the timeline was fluid and a bit more forgiving than I'd first feared. We had time to complete the manuscript. To be successful and produce something that we could both be proud of, we would need every minute the publisher could give us.

In the months leading up to this, Jennifer and I had had several vulnerable and transparent conversations about where her work was and her plans to bring it more fully into the world.

Lucky for us, it turns out that the mountains of Western North Carolina—where we've made our home, above the density of what's going on in the world—have some magical powers.

Jennifer and I started to navigate the complex task of converting her unedited video transcripts into a cohesive narrative for everyone else who isn't part of her community. Her people already get her. They appreciate and celebrate her way of explaining complex concepts. However, I became more agitated the deeper we dug.

Such was my anxiety that at some point every day, I would first respectfully knock on her office door, then barge in without waiting for a reply. I had questions, dammit, and they required answers.

The unassailable truth is that I was struggling emotionally. If I didn't figure out why, I would soon become an impediment to the process instead of Jennifer's snappily dressed salvation, stepping in at the last minute to employ my secret weapon: creating order out of chaos.

It's something to behold, even if I do say so myself.

It's not that the actual process of reorganizing Jennifer's thoughts and ideas onto the page was unpleasant, per se. Initially, there were some discussions to uncover her intent for each chapter, clarifying the Brain Bridge of each story. She was focused on building a deeper understanding of our default operating system and changing it into one of more flow and less stress.

I quickly accessed the project's portal in the quantum field, the third entity called **UN**STUCK. I understand the language and have lived this reality for twelve years. For me, writing soon became a welcome joy, regardless of the nagging feeling of imminent danger nipping at the back of my neck, just out of reach.

I realized that I hadn't written anything of any consequence since the last book I published over four years earlier, and nothing since then under the motivation of a deadline. Day after day, I gave myself over to the practical application of my craft, as any journeyman would. I found it soothing to slow down and drop into the vortex of the third entity, where all the right words waited for me.

I built up paragraphs, then pages, and eventually chapters one word at a time. It felt good to be in partnership with Jennifer toward a common goal. I'll admit it; it felt good to be of use to my sweetie.

But while writing the book, I started not enjoying myself. In one particularly challenging session where I was seeking clarity around a couple of concepts that seemed to contradict themselves, I got pissed off because I felt like I wasn't communicating in a way that she could hear me. The entire enterprise started to taste bittersweet. I knew I was sabotaging myself and the project simultaneously but couldn't find the energy to give a damn.

"Why?" Jennifer asked, frustrated with my bullshit, not to mention my curt answers. "Why are you depressed?"

"I don't know," I offered unconvincingly.

"Good thing you have a coaching call today," she said.

"Shit," I thought, "Wini."

In the seventy-five minutes that I worked with Wini Curley, an intuitive of epic proportions, she asked questions that had me going deep, despite my resignation and doubt. She started the ball rolling by asking me, "Adam, how are you today?" Wini is a sneaky coach.

The spoken-word salad that came tumbling out of my mouth woke up synapses in my brain, which started to fire and wire together. I heard myself saying things with which I hadn't previously connected. I was so engrossed in speaking that there was no time for shame at my admissions.

Once, I'd explained to Jennifer that in my most triggered states when I was disconnected from our third entity and my higher self, my ever-sneaky self-critic, Sluggo, would act as a filter, collecting small bits of information, words, and expressions, separating them from the main body of our conversations to use in my defense later.

I would then use them, shamefully, as an emotional weapon in defense of my manhood, honor, or some other bullshit concept of masculinity I had adopted along my journey, in place of the truth of who I really am.

Hey, I didn't say I was proud of it. At least I called myself out on this weak-kneed tactic and confessed to Jennifer. Not that it took the sting out of any of the things I'd already said to her in anger. Shit. Throw me a bone, will ya?

The capacity to stash away tree-shaking information isn't all bad—it seems I have a head for remembering strange and useless factoids.

One of the fascinating ones was a comment that Jennifer had made to me about six months earlier.

In a moment of courageous transparency, she'd admitted to me that a part of her was scared to write a book. While she knew that it was important for her mission to assist as many people as possible, she knew that in publishing the book, she'd be asked to show up in a more significant way.

There was still a little girl inside her that didn't want to be called out, ridiculed, or be taken down by doubters and critics. My experience of sharing intimate details about my journey in the printed form, such as drug use, had sensitized me to how easy it is for someone to take your words and turn them around for their benefit. Once your story is out in public, it can't be called back.

I hadn't understood before speaking with Wini that I'd subconsciously taken on Jennifer's fear. I wasn't even aware of how it affected my participation in the project. I had become demanding and bombastic because I wanted to protect her. I didn't want her to regret telling the whole world, including her parents, that she sees and interprets things differently than most people do.

In that moment of revelation, I had to admit out loud to Wini that I was carrying Jennifer and believed that she wasn't up to the task of accurately articulating her vision of harmony for humanity. Without even knowing it, I had held her as small.

All I heard while I was speaking was the beginning riffs of the Beastie Boys song "Sabotage" blasting in my head.

As if all of this wasn't enough for one coaching session, Sluggo unveiled one last surprise to me, sumbitch. It seems that when Jennifer asked me to help her to translate her programs into words, and after getting in the rhythm and enjoying the flow, I had somehow made up that this was going to be *my* book.

Wini sat silently on the other end of our Zoom call as I dug my own grave with my words. When I stopped rambling, she looked at me with compassion. Before I could judge my judgment and put myself in the barrel, she smiled at me. She held my gaze until my shoulders slumped, and I gave up the ghost.

I returned the smile sheepishly. "Um, Wini?" I started. "I think I have an apology to make."

"Maybe," she offered. "Maybe you just want to tell Jennifer how thankful you are for this wonderful opportunity for discovery?"

"Yeah," I thought as I woodenly nodded to myself, "that feels better."

After a pause in the conversation where I searched for the right words to express my gratitude for all she had done for me in the coaching session, I softly said, "Thank you, Wini. I love you."

"I love you too, Adam," and then she was gone.

It took me a few minutes to summon up the courage to talk to Jennifer. I explained to her what I had just experienced and the clarity that it provided me. She was grateful, she said, for Wini and how she had shown up for me. And then she thanked me for being so vulnerable. We hugged for what felt like a long time.

"Jennifer, this is your book. I trust your instincts about how you want this to be communicated. I'll do what I do, then it'll be your call on what it looks and reads like from there. I'm just happy to be in partnership with you on this. If I can do this, then I know that I'll finally be able to finish the book I've started."

We both laughed at that. My book is a science-fiction story I started writing many years ago, and it's so big and complex it scared the crap out of me. I became convinced it would never be completed.

Now I know better.

I'll first have to assist Jennifer in completing this book, but at least I can do so now, letting love win. I can finally release my attachment to its outcome and enjoy the process. It feels great to be free of the weight around my neck of carrying her, the project, and anyone who will read this. On this one, I can let her take the load knowing that she's got this—this, and oh so much more.

I might even do a little dance before I go back in and get busy writing again. And I might even start writing down some ideas for my next book. Stay tuned.

The Ingredients to Transcend the Whole Paradigm of Self-Sabotage So You Can Dance with It All

Adam's story is a perfect example of listening to the dissonance within and taking action. That's all the feeling of self-sabotage is. So why don't we just start relating to it that way? Your timing is not necessarily cosmic-perfect timing, so are you sabotaging yourself or just being asked to consider that you might need to have a conversation or take some action before your project or dream can come alive?

It feels to me more like Life is giving you discomfort to be able to look at the actions you need to take to get back into congruence with your flow.

We don't need any more excuses to judge ourselves.

In Adam's case, he wasn't sabotaging himself; he was doing something he had never done before with me and hadn't realized there were things he didn't know he didn't know. Then he got the information he needed, and off we went to the races.

I appreciate him for listening to that little whisper sooner rather than later.

Once you transcend the idea of self-sabotage and start dancing with the opportunities that Life brings you, you realize that your enjoyment isn't conditional on you completely understanding the steps. It's not predicated on the left brain or right brain, logical or creative. All of it comes together at the same time. It's experiential.

An appropriate analogy would be the initial scary feeling when learn how to ride a bike. Once you're on the bike and the training wheels come off, at some point, even though you wobble a bit, you build just enough momentum to be able to control the direction of the bike, then off you go!

Consider for a moment that, at first, your mastery of the dance isn't as important as your willingness to go along and enjoy the ride.

So how do you know when you're in a dance with all of Creation? It's when you start playing with Life as though it's an adventure into the unknown that can only have outcomes that assist you. Don't be surprised when everything you've put into motion starts to slow down or ceases to move at all. It will all wait for you to recalibrate to a frequency of delight and appreciation, but the longer you take to get into your heart, the harder it will be to get it all moving again.

Slow down to speed up, and don't worry; you aren't sabotaging yourself. Your ship keeps coming in.

Action Steps

In our Get Out of Your Own Way™ program, we've created some great practices that will help you stay in the flow.

One of them is called Zero Pointing Yourself, which helps you transcend all judgment from so-called self-sabotage. You can find the link here: https://thewideawakening.com/unstuck-resources. The exercise takes only about ten minutes, and it will reset your entire frequency, making you a magnet for great ideas and delightful synchronicities.

Do this every morning for the next week and see how you feel. If you like it, do it forever. It's so much easier to prevent problems than to deal with going off track later.

CHAPTER 13

TRANSCENDING SELF-DOUBT

*"If you hear a voice within you saying you
cannot paint, then by all means paint,
and that voice will be silenced."*
Vincent van Gogh

According to Merriam-Webster, the definition of transcend is:

1. To rise above or go beyond the limits of something.
2. To triumph over the negative or restrictive aspects of something.
3. To be before, beyond, and above (the universe or material existence).
4. To outstrip or outdo some attribute, quality, or power.

Whether we consider it, entertain it, or suffer from it, self-doubt is a well-practiced part of the human condition. Who among us hasn't had, at one time or another, doubt or concern about a looming decision, be it a first date, marriage, divorce, a business proposal, or a financial calculation?

For some people, doubt can be a powerful tool when used with precision and governed by boundaries. For others, doubt becomes the basic assumption of their operating system, leaving them so unsure that they question every decision they make, resulting in low self-esteem.

Otherwise intelligent, capable people will often attribute their successes to outside forces such as luck, market conditions, or fate. They'll deflect or minimize any praise or acknowledgment because they don't feel worthy of it, often without any evidence to the contrary.

Here's what I know.

The only constant in a creation-based Universe is change. We are in that Universe and were born to create. By definition, we are creating based on what we've experienced that we know. That which we are creating is not known. Our vision is unknown until it's made manifest in 3D.

Is it possible that doubt is simply a misinterpretation of the energy of anticipation that our greater self is feeling? Perhaps the feeling of doubt is more accurately described as the feeling humans have when they're trying to survive and they're presented with a situation or project they don't know how to handle. From a thriving perspective, when you're going direct with your innate wisdom, that same energy is interpreted as exhilaration for the adventure into the unknown.

That should be approached with childlike curiosity, not fear and protection.

The title of this chapter is not "Managing Self-Doubt," and that's deliberate.

Our 3D solution is also subject to the first law of thermodynamics, which effectively says that you can't get more energy out than you put in. This is just a fancy way of saying that to transcend self-doubt, we need to deploy a higher mind or frequency of thought than the mind that created it.

So, we have to go quantum. Instead of matter trying to influence matter, let's go direct by having energy influence energy in the fifth dimension, where all possibilities exist.

When you do that, you haven't banished self-doubt; you've risen above it. And in the paradigm shift that I described above, we get to rise above it. Reinterpret your doubt from the place of your thriving mind rather than just the 3D surviving mind.

You can go kicking and screaming, or you can just go.

"Doubting,"
Written by Adam Lamb, about Amy Card's story

"In a society that profits from your self-doubt, liking yourself is a rebellious act."
Caroline Caldwell

The airport was disorganized. Weary travelers were hounding the ticket agents, trying to rebook flights, and people mobbed the rental car desks trying to get the attention of the harried customer service reps.

Earlier in the day, the airlines had started to cancel flights due to a wave of severe weather across the northeast, and as a result, I'd missed my connecting flight. I was twelve hours behind schedule. By the time I got to Albany, it felt like I was pushing a noodle up a hill.

Jennifer was going to have to start without me.

"Amy, I think you should come to the Omega Institute and help me work the room," Jennifer had announced at a team meeting three weeks before the event.

"Work the room?" I thought to myself. "What does that mean?"

"Um, yeah, sure," I stammered. I wasn't going to fuss about it in front of the team. Still, I was frustrated that my boss put me on the spot without giving me prior knowledge of the ask. We hadn't discussed it in our weekly one-on-one, so her statement caught me completely off guard.

Once the meeting ended, I called Jennifer. "Hey," I started, "I didn't want to say anything at the meeting, but are you asking me or telling me to join you in New York?" I'm sure she could hear the annoyance in my voice. I continued, "It would have been nice to have a little warning, you know?"

She agreed with me and explained that her higher levels had told her during her morning communion with them that it would be a good thing for me to go. "Of course, I'm asking you, Amy. I would never tell you that you *had* to go."

"Although," Jennifer continued, "if you feel the contraction or expansion, you'll know." Doing what Life is presenting me, ugh. I still didn't know if I completely understood what that meant.

"Okay, okay," I told her, "I'll let you know tomorrow if I can make it happen."

Everything seemed to fall into place during the next week, and suddenly, it looked easy to travel to Rhinebeck, New York.

Doing a presentation at the Omega Institute was no small thing. I had seen Jennifer on stage in front of a live audience before, and as soon as the stage lights hit her, she owned the room. Jennifer loves people. She was always funny, relaxed, and sincere when she spoke. Her audience was always enthusiastic and appreciative. More than once, I caught myself thinking, "How the hell does she do that? She's got them leaning forward in their chairs, all in."

"I could never be that good." Big sigh.

It wasn't the first time a thought like that had crossed my mind. As far back as I can remember, even as a kid, I'd never felt confident. The opinions of other people mattered more to me, for some reason. I once cut my hair short because a friend said I should. My mother was furious, but I wanted my friend to like me, so I never considered disagreeing with her.

I wasn't a bad student or anything like that; it's just that compared to the few friends I had, I didn't know who I was or what I could be. They all had strong ideas about where they were going in life. They acted assertive and self-assured, and they had it all together. One was a gifted athlete; the other had an amazing musical talent. As far as I knew, I had no talent or gift. It was just me.

I became fascinated with self-development work and took classes in different disciplines. I even took coaching classes with Jennifer at The Wide Awakening. After completing the Awakened Coach training program, I accepted a position with the company.

I focused on ensuring that we delivered on our commitments to our clients by working on the travel, hotel bookings, and organizational details. I was good at my job.

I supported the other team members in the background, so I was surprised when Jennifer asked me to help her during her presentation at The Omega Institute. I wasn't familiar with what that would be like because I stayed mainly within the wheelhouse of my immediate duties.

I was worried that I would do a bad job and embarrass Jennifer in front of this important audience. She didn't seem too concerned as she replied, "We have checklists; you'll do great."

I waited for a solution to present in the Albany airport since I'd missed my shuttle bus to Rhinebeck. I'll admit that I was a little relieved when the older man working the information kiosk confirmed that I was indeed stranded at the airport without an obvious way forward.

Jennifer had a friend with her at the institute, so she already had support. In four hours, she would take the stage. I wasn't sure what more value I could offer, even if I could get there.

I called to give her the unwelcome news. My shoulders and neck felt tight, and I started to have stomach pains. I suddenly felt very small.

"Jennifer, it's Amy," I began. I told her how the travel day from hell had unfolded and that I was stuck in Albany. It was highly likely that I wouldn't make it to the Omega Institute; nothing was presenting.

"What do you mean nothing is presenting, Amy? What have you tried?" she replied.

"I've been waiting for something to *present*," I said meekly.

"Amy, you've got to take action on the adventure to *see* what presents. Your cosmic entourage can't respond with a dance step unless *you* take a dance step." She then asked me, "Have you checked to see if the rental companies have any cars available?"

"They've been so busy; I didn't bother to ask."

"If you never try, you'll never know what's possible," Jennifer said.

"Christina's there with you, right?" I asked. "She can help you."

"Amy," Jennifer took a deep breath. "Christina is not you. Don't be a delightful bonehead; get a car and get up here. I need you." I didn't say a word. Jennifer continued, "Remember that the answer is always yes until it's a number That's the only way you'll know for sure what is presenting."

Resigned to a futile and exasperating fiasco, I hung up without saying goodbye.

I walked up to the Avis counter. I was fifth in line. At that moment, breathing in deeply, I committed to getting to the institute, regardless of which rabbit hole I had to go down.

Before I could take my backpack off, a representative who hadn't been there when I walked up waved me forward. They upgraded me to a luxury car at no extra charge because that's all they had left. Within fifteen minutes, I had completed the paperwork and paid for the rental and was sitting on a deliciously warm seat in a beautiful preheated car, gripping the heated steering wheel, and on my way to Rhinebeck.

Before leaving Albany, I stopped to grab a coffee. When I pulled up to the window to pay, the attendant told me that the car in front of me had paid for my drink.

Free coffee? Yes, please. "Now, this feels expansive." I sighed as I stretched out my legs and settled into my seat. I turned on the stereo and started listening to the audiobook I'd brought with me about a new modality I was interested in, *Soul Realignment*.

As I drove, I lost myself in the audiobook. Time dissolved like the snow slowly evaporating on the warming roadway.

Before I knew it, I was pulling into the parking lot of The Omega Institute. Jennifer greeted me with a big hug as I got out of the car.

After returning home, I realized what an amazing time I'd had working with Jennifer and our audience. It all unfolded smoothly and effortlessly. And I enjoyed meeting the people who took a leap of faith and registered for our next program.

I was excited for them and became uncharacteristically invested in their success.

Settling back in at home, I felt strangely enriched. I was so glad I went. I understood in a way I previously never could without going through the experience that I would never have gotten there if I hadn't finally decided to investigate what was possible and act on what was *actually presenting.*

It was so much more satisfying than sitting on my hands waiting for the Universe to come to me.

I've grown so much since that weekend. I now know I have gifts and talents that make me a unique expression of Creation and a piece of the puzzle of Heaven on Earth.

I owe Jennifer and Jeannie (on The Wide Awakening team) a special debt of gratitude. They deliberately created and continue to maintain a space of neutrality at The Wide Awakening in which I first explored and then developed and practiced my abilities without judgment or fear. They became valued partners in my journey of self-discovery and witnessed my self-actualization.

Because of them, as well as the other team members of The Wide Awakening, our clients, my coaches, my mentors, and the work I dedicated myself to, I no longer give any attention or energy to the opinions or judgments of anyone else. Empowered by that, I've cultivated a feeling of grounded confidence that encourages me to be consistently who I really am for those I love and serve.

Thank you.

What Ingredients Are Needed to Transcend Self-Doubt?

It takes practice to do what Life is presenting you. The amount of time we spend discounting our intuition with logic is astounding to me still. We master the art of reading the expansive or contractive feelings we have. In the end, true mastery has you not even needing to feel expansion or contraction—eventually, you just do it, like riding a bike. Mastery takes time.

You have 37 trillion cells, all connected to your greater wisdom. This ingredient just is; there's nothing to do about it.

You can go kicking and screaming, or you can just go. The mental rationales and emotional gymnastics are all very entertaining, but in the end, what Life is presenting you is just what it is. Act on it, and based on what happens, you'll discover which direction to go.

Reinterpret the energy of self-doubt. You aren't really doubting yourself; you're simply being presented with something you're not experienced with yet, and you need some training, input, information, insight, or support. So go get it instead of judging yourself (unless you want to just keep surviving, of course!).

Make sure you have a community of people who are thriving alongside you so you can have them remind you who you are and why you're here when you forget. To explore your options and become a member of the Heaven on Earth Construction Crew I invite you to visit https://thewideawakening.com/ .

Action Steps

For this chapter, you have a simple task. Explore opportunities for connection by visiting https://thewideawakening.com/ .

Be loved and supported.

And jump into our The Thriving Operating System program if it calls you to find fulfillment and meaning on purpose while you're enjoying your abundance. It would be an honor to be part of your journey.

BRINGING IT ALL TOGETHER

"What you seek is seeking you."

Rumi

Both of my parents have had cancer.

When my mother had cancer, she asked me what I "saw" about it. Instead of telling her anything, I asked her a simple question: "What do you think causes you the most stress?"

She responded, "Well, I love you, so I worry about you. That's what you do when you're a parent."

I told my mom that love and worry are not the same things. In fact, worry is a form of carrying the weight of the world. The underlying implication of worry is that we're uncomfortable with the idea that we have no control over a person or situation and that we don't fully trust that they will find their own way.

My mom thought about that for a while. Then she said, at that point, her belief was just too well practiced. I disagreed. And I said that this way of thinking was not helping her health. She said that if I called her more, that would help her peace of mind.

So, I call her more. I'm glad she asked me to because I love talking to my mom and dad.

Love is love. Worry is worry. Love and worry are completely separate things.

Fortunately, both of my parents made it through cancer treatments, although neither of them enjoys aging that much. They continue to be net contributors to their communities and great human beings.

They are not, however, enjoying what is happening in the world right now. My mother, in particular, I have witnessed, has been traumatized from witnessing the pain, division, and judgment we are inflicting on each other on multiple issues.

I know that she's not alone.

Suffering only remains if we don't take the emotional energy and turn it into action. I've become adept at taking the polarity and contrast in this world and using the emotional energy generated in my body about recent events to fuel my passion for becoming fulfilled, learning more about who we are and what we're capable of, and paying it forward into the world.

I've noticed that many people are frustrated because they want to contribute to building a bridge for humanity to walk across instead of trying to fix all the walls that have been erected. For me, fixing walls is a waste of time.

I go back to one of Bucky Fuller's quotes: "You never change things by fighting the existing reality. To change something, build a new model that makes the existing model obsolete."

These days, many have lost their loved ones without saying goodbye. I'm sure the trauma and sadness that come from that are so difficult to bear, and I'm hugely grateful that my parents are still with us.

In my experience, most people don't have their confidence, hope, energy, or sense of self intact enough to take inspired action. They are scared or overwhelmed, or they've lost hope. I feel that myself occasionally.

The chapters, exercises, and Brain Bridges in this book are not just theories. I have worked with all of the concepts with tens of thousands of people, and the work has been essential for me to be able to not only stay sane but also to make a difference, be catalyzed to assist others, and evolve our programs to address the important life questions that are coming up for people.

Why? Because my training, experience, and instincts tell me that it's possible for us to create a world where we don't judge, separate from, or kill each other in attempts to fix the past and instead build a world where we can all find a part to play meaningfully. Because many people from all walks of life have barely been able to survive, let alone thrive, and it doesn't have to be that way. Meaning and contribution are available to everyone—they just need to know how to be superpowered.

Because we can thrive together, but we must first understand the Thriving Operating System individually and start living that way. Otherwise, we'll spend all of eternity arguing about how someone else is taking our power away. When you experience all of the power you have, nobody can take it away.

To that end, please join me in our community, Agents of Awakening—that's where it's all happening. Maybe it's time for you to take The Thriving Operating Systems 1 and 2 with our Wide Awakening Team and me because it's just time.

I trust that you'll know exactly what to do after reading the book to this point and doing the exercises.

Something I know for sure: the magic that occurred to complete this book was a team effort. It was a completion for me, true healing of *independence disease*. Ten years ago, I would never have called in all the earth angels that assisted me in getting this done, or at very least, I would have rejected much of the help that I received. Writing this book was an example of everything that we talked about, lived through the experience. I even had an editor named Kay who could edit overnight while I slept, who showed up only a few weeks before for a different reason. If I had solely gone with North American editors, again, I wouldn't have met the due date. I could tell you oodles of other events that occurred completely due to getting out of the way of the entire Universe so that things could flow.

One of those little miracles was Adam being available to help me write the book.

The first time I put pen to paper on this book was in Maui with Adam on our second big date. The last time I'll put pen to paper on this book is with Adam in our home, as he transcribes the program that this came from and my editors and I create from what he transcribes.

I am so grateful for this journey with Adam, for everyone on my team and in The Wide Awakening, for your courage to remember who you really are, and for all of the future alchemy that will happen in our lives and in humanity as this book goes out into the world.

From my heart, thank you for being in the Heaven on Earth Construction Crew. Don't carry yourself or this earth; just enjoy the becoming.

Inevitably, we will all be unstuck and get out of the Universe's way when our spirits leave these bodies. Yet we came here to "live the most fulfilling life and make the biggest impact while experiencing meaning and using our superpowers to the fullest" while we are alive.

My deepest desire is that you know it's possible to thrive, that you will take steps in that direction, and that you will thrive in this lifetime.

With love,
Jennifer

ABOUT THE AUTHOR

Jennifer Hough was a corporate economist for a large multinational company until she got physically sick (migraines, depression and fibromyalgia) from toxic exposure, and watched her life fall into effort and struggle. She then traveled the world and worked with scientists, doctors, mystics and spiritual leaders, who corroborated the tie between our vitality, our abundance, our ability to flow and the laws of physics. As a result of this work she made an astounding full recovery.

Her joy is to take her clients on an experiential journey into the use of everyday physics to shift their ability to flourish in business, health, and abundance. Jennifer's work has been featured in documentaries, TV, radio, best-selling books, and on stages around the world. Jennifer has 20 years of experience educating doctors (MDs, NDs and DCs), teachers, CEOs and Associations (Nurses, NDs, HR, Native American) in the physics of flow through her program, Get Out of Your Own Way™. She is a 5 Time Best Selling Author and contributor to over 11 books on health, fulfillment and applied physics

Printed in Great Britain
by Amazon